A Chronology of
The United Nations
1941—1958

Waldo Chamberlin

Thomas Hovet, Jr.

Richard N. Swift

with a preface by
Andrew W. Cordier
Executive Assistant to the
Secretary-General of the United Nations

Oceana Publications, Inc.
New York
1959

JX
1977
.C483

© Copyright, 1959, by Oceana Publications, Inc.
All Rights Reserved

Library of Congress Catalog Card Number 59-14270

Printed in the United States of America

PREFACE

The lengthening experience of the United Nations, as well as the importance and wide scope of its activities, provides ample justification for this chronology of United Nations events. In fact the author, Professor Waldo Chamberlin of New York University, has placed all scholars and students of the United Nations in his debt by providing a useful list of significant events from the origins of the United Nations to the present. By now the number of events is myriad and the process of selection was not easy. But the author has succeeded in listing the events that have special importance and also are most frequently referred to in scholarly treatises, speeches and discussions on the United Nations.

The comparatively short life of the United Nations already provides opportunity for the assessment of certain trends. Whether these trends are temporary or permanent, only the future will determine.

The Charter as drafted at Dumbarton Oaks and San Francisco in 1944 and 1945, although a written and well-defined instrument, is like all other constitutions or basic laws a changing instrument. It has demonstrated its flexibility and its capacity to adjust to changing situations.

On the negative side, the Charter has operated in a period of such tension and strain as to make some of its provisions temporarily inoperative. On the positive side, the very nature of the world emergency and of the opportunities for other forms of concerted action have given some provisions of the Charter a fullness of meaning and application which was not anticipated at the time when they were drafted.

The Charter was drawn up on the assumption of the continuing prevalence of a substantial degree of great power cooperation. The Second World War had been conducted on the basis of the cooperation of the Grand Alliance, and the conditions which underlay this Alliance, it was presumed, would continue into the era of peace. Thus the rule of unanimity applicable to the permanent members of the Security Council—a rule warmly endorsed by the Great Powers themselves—was regarded as a guarantee that the interest of world peace and security would be constantly safeguarded.

A corollary to the voting arrangements in the Security Council were the provisions establishing a Military Staff Committee with responsibility for the direction of military forces in the interest of peace.

But both of these concepts, requiring for their effective implementation substanial solidarity among the Great Powers in the interest of keeping the peace, soon vanished. Tension between east and west replaced cooperation, and firm irreconcilable positions in the Security Council were reflected either by permanent members joining with other permanent members and non-permanent members to establish a majority, or by a minority through the exercise of the veto. This political atmosphere was also reflected in the stultification of the work of the Military Staff Committee.

This tension, popularly called the "cold war," however was relieved on one important issue by action within the United Nations. It is a striking fact that more than half of the so-called vetoes registered were those relating to votes on applications for membership in the United Nations. After agreement had been reached in 1955 among the Great Powers on a generally acceptable formula, the great majority of the applicants were admitted unanimously. It is not excluded that other issues in the cold war may find a solution through this type of negotiation among the Great Powers and within the framework of the United Nations.

In addition, the tension among the Great Powers has led to an intensification of the development of processes of mediation and conciliation and to the adaptation of special administrative mechanisms for ending disputes and reducing tensions. Thus, arrangements endorsed by the General Assembly included the presence of the United Nations Emergency Force on the Armistice Demarcation Line between Egypt and Israel, the establishment last year of a United Nations Observation Group in Lebanon, and of the United Nations presence in Jordan. Through provisions of the Armistice Agreements and through action of the Security Council, a United Nations Truce Supervision Organization exists in Palestine. A United Nations Military Observer Group functions in India and Pakistan, United Nations action in Korea in 1950 and in the Suez crisis in 1956 blocked the way to general war, and the quiet processes of mediation and conciliation have worked effectively in many others, though perhaps less dramatic, circumstances.

A powerful force in support of these positive efforts for peace has been the concerted support of the middle-sized and small powers who represent a majority of the membership of the United Nations. These powers find their influence best and most effectively expressed through the United Nations. Here their voice is heard; here it has meaning; here it can be combined with other voices to constitute an effective third force that has often carried the day in world policy.

Individually, they do not possess the advantages or disadvantages of power. That belongs to the Great Powers. The power politics of the Great Powers gives all of these middle-sized and smaller powers a vested interest of concern in the outcome of the diplomatic problems, the tensions, and the external policies of the Great Powers. In the sheer interest of self-preservation they find it necessary collectively to help contain the rivalries of the Great Powers, and to bring brush fires of smaller countries to an end before they attract the fuses of Great Power involvement.

Another striking trend in world politics, which has been dramatically reflected in the United Nations, is the speed with which colonial and non-self-governing territories have attained their independence. At San Francisco. during the drafting of the United Nations Charter, it was almost universally assumed that the blueprint for trusteeship, Chapter 12 of the Charter, would have relevance for a generation or two. After only thirteen short years, trust territories have been reduced in number by their transformation to independence and steps are now being considered in the United Nations, with the early reduction of the number of administering members, as to how the Trusteeship Council can be reduced in the number of its members. Furthermore, the number of non-self-governing territories has been reduced in the same period from 76 to 49. This rapid transformation of peoples from colonial or non-self-governing status to that of independence is having a transforming effect upon the United Nations in relation to them. It is symbolized by the enlargement of the scope of the political and economic tasks and responsibility of the United Nations for these large areas of the world.

These major adaptations and trends in the United Nations demonstrate its capacity for flexible adjustment to emergencies as well as to the requirements of political change and economic growth. They demonstrate that the United Nations is, in fact, a major force for peace and an effective instrument for the promotion of the economic and social progress of mankind.

ANDREW W. CORDIER

ABBREVIATIONS

ACC	Administrative Committee on Coordination
AEC	Atomic Energy Commission
ECAFE	Economic Commission for Asia and the Far East
ECE	Economic Commission for Europe
ECLA	Economic Commission for Latin America
GATT	General Agreement on Tariffs and Trade
IAEA	International Atomic Energy Agency
IBRD	International Bank for Reconstruction and Development
ICJ	International Court of Justice
IFC	International Finance Corporation
IMCO	International Maritime Consultative Organization
IMF	International Monetary Fund
ITU	International Telecommunications Union
NNRP	Neutral Nations Repatriation Commission
NNSC	Neutral Nations Supervisory Commission
OTC	Office for Trade Co-operation
SUNFED	Special United Nations Fund for Economic Development
UAR	United Arab Republic
UK	United Kingdom
UN	United Nations
UNCOK	United Nations Commission for Korea
UNCURK	United Nations Commission for the Unification and Rehabilitation of Korea
UNEF	United Nations Emergency Force
UNICEF	United Nations International Children's Emergency Fund and United Nations Children's Fund
UNKRA	United Nations Korean Reconstruction Agency
UNOGIL	United Nations Observer Group in Lebanon
UNRPR	United Nations Relief for Palestine Refugees
UNRWAPRNE	United Nations Relief and Works Agency for Palestine Refugees in the Near East
UNSCOB	United Nations Special Committee on the Balkans
UNSCOP	United Nations Special Committee on Palestine
UNTCOK	United Nations Temporary Commission on Korea
UPU	Universal Postal Union
US	United States
USSR	Union of Soviet Socialist Republics

INTRODUCTION

The United Nations is almost fifteen years old and the extent and range of its activities during that period has been so vast that it is difficult, and often impossible, to remember when a particular event took place. It is even more difficult to recall what else was transpiring in the United Nations at the moment a particular event occurred. In our research we have found a constant need for a handy guide such as this, particularly since 1952 when the Secretariat of the United Nations discontinued its mimeographed chronology.

This *Chronology* enables a reader to see what was going on in the United Nations at any time; the index enables him to trace the development under a particular entry (see for example, "Human rights" or "Palestine.")

Anyone who follows the development of the United Nations will be aware of the problem of selection of significant events from among those of an organization that holds about two thousand meetings and produces approximately forty thousand documents (in English) each year. The choice of events for inclusion herein was determined by what we thought would most likely be important to most readers and that could be contained in a convenient, inexpensive little book of about fifty pages. Thus the Chronology is not intended to meet the demands of the specialist concerning events in his particular field.

In the area of administration, for example, we have included what we consider to be the most important action each year—the authorization of funds for the budget (see December 21, 1952 on page 25). We have not, however, included such events concerning the evolution of personnel policy as those that preceded and followed the July 13, 1954 advisory opinion of the International Court of Justice on the awards of the Administrative Tribunal. Our reasoning in this instance was that the Brooklyn Grand Jury presentment of December 2, 1952 and the President's Executive Order of January 9, 1953 were actions by the United States and not by the United Nations. In addition, both of these steps, like the Committee of Jurists Report of January 30, 1953 and the General Assembly's revision of the Staff Rules and the Statute of the Administrative Tribunal on December 9, 1953 were less important than the advisory opinion of the Court and, therefore, of interest primarily to the relatively small, even though important, group of students of international administration (among whom we wish to be numbered). Similarly, the General Assembly's revision of the Statute of the Administrative Tribunal on November 8, 1955, in view of the lack of enthusiasm on the part of virtually all delegations, seems to us to have been less important for the United Nations than for the United States. Therefore, we have excluded from the *Chronology* all items except that which, in our opinion, was the most important step in this series of events relating to the evolution of personnel policy—the advisory opinion of the Court.

All the vetoes in the Security Council have been listed, even though many were relatively unimportant, because of the general interest in this subject. We believe that we are justified in concluding as a "presumed veto" the result of the September 24, 1947 private meeting of the Council on the question of a governor for Trieste. Certain seemingly relatively minor events have been included when, in our judgment, they indicate important changes in United Nations policy or development. The increasing activity of the organization in the field of international commodity arrangements is an example and accounts for the entries in 1950, 1954, 1955 and 1958 (see Index, p. 40). Such selectivity represents a subjective judgment but we consider it very significant that the United Nations appears to be moving into the field of international commodity arrangements, hitherto the province of other international organizations and *ad hoc* conferences. In this instance our selection of events is intended to draw attention to what may be an important trend in the growth of the United Nations.

WALDO CHAMBERLIN
THOMAS HOVET, JR.
RICHARD N. SWIFT

CHRONOLOGY OF
THE UNITED NATIONS
1941 - 1958

1941

Aug. 14

ATLANTIC CHARTER: statement of principles to govern the establishment of a world-wide system of security

1942

Jan. 1

DECLARATION BY UNITED NATIONS: statement supporting Atlantic Charter, signed by 26 nations

1943

Oct. 30

MOSCOW DECLARATION: necessity for an international organization agreed upon by China, USSR, UK and US

1944

May 1 - 17

COMMONWEALTH PRIME MINISTERS MEETING: agreement that UK should discuss plans for an international organization with signers of Moscow Declaration

Oct. 9

DUMBARTON OAKS PROPOSALS: recommendation concerning the establishment of an international organization: August 21 to September 29 USSR, UK and US negotiations; September 29 to October 7 China, UK and US negotiations

Nov. 1 - 6

WELLINGTON CONFERENCE: Australia and New Zealand approved twelve resolutions in a general international organization

1945

Jan. 30 - Feb. 2	MALTA CONFERENCE: U.K. and U.S. meetings prior to Yalta Conference
Feb. 4 - 11	YALTA CONFERENCE: U.S.S.R., U.K. and U.S. agreed on Security Council voting formula
Feb. 21 - March 8	INTER-AMERICAN CONFERENCE ON PROBLEMS OF WAR AND PEACE: American republics, except Argentina, met and agreed that Dumbarton Oaks proposals constituted basis for an organization (Mexico City)
April 4 - 13	BRITISH COMMONWEALTH MEETING: agreed that Dumbarton Oaks proposals provided base for an organization
April 9 - 20	COMMITTEE OF JURISTS: jurists from 44 nations drafted statute for an International Court of Justice
April 9 - June 25	U.N. CONFERENCE ON INTERNATIONAL ORGANIZATION: representatives from 50 nations drafted Charter
June 7	SECURITY COUNCIL: Statement by the Delegations of the Four Sponsoring Governments on Voting Procedures in the Security Council
June 26	CHARTER: signed by representatives of 50 nations
June 27	PREPARATORY COMMISSION OF THE U.N.: 1st meeting
July 6	CHARTER: 1st ratification by Nicaragua
Aug. 6	ATOMIC ENERGY: Hiroshima bomb
Aug. 8	CHARTER: deposit of 1st ratification by U.S.
Aug. 16 - Nov. 24	PREPARATORY COMMISSION: meetings of the Executive Committee
Oct. 24	CHARTER: came into force with deposit of U.S.S.R. instrument of ratification
Nov. 15	ATOMIC ENERGY: Canada, U.K. and U.S. agreed on establishment of U.N. atomic energy commission
Nov. 24 - Dec. 23	PREPARATORY COMMISSION: second session
Dec. 16 - 26	ATOMIC ENERGY: Council of Foreign Ministers of U.S.S.R., U.K. and U.S. agreed on establishment of U.N. commission on atomic energy

1946

Jan. 10 - Feb. 14	GENERAL ASSEMBLY: 1st session part one
Jan. 17	SECURITY COUNCIL: 1st meeting
Jan. 19	IRAN: 1st dispute brought to Security Council; presence of U.S.S.R. troops in Iran
Jan. 21	GREECE: presence of British troops brought to Security Council by U.S.S.R.
Jan. 21	INDONESIA: presence of British troops brought to Security Council of the Ukraine
Jan. 23 - Feb. 18	ECONOMIC AND SOCIAL COUNCIL: 1st session
Jan. 24	ATOMIC ENERGY: establishment of U.N. Atomic Energy Commission by General Assembly
Jan. 25	MEMBERSHIP: Albania applied
Feb. 1	SECRETARY-GENERAL: Trygve Lie appointed
Feb. 4	MILITARY STAFF COMMITTEE: 1st meeting
Feb. 4	SYRIA-LEBANON: presence of French-British troops brought to Security Council by Syria and Lebanon
Feb. 6	COURT: 1st judges of the International Court of Justice elected

1946 (Continued)

Feb. 9	NON-SELF-GOVERNING TERRITORIES: Secretary-General requested by General Assembly to include in his annual report summaries of information received
Feb. 14	HEADQUARTERS: New York chosen by General Assembly as interim headquarters
Feb. 16	NARCOTIC DRUGS: Economic and Social Council established Commission on Narcotic Drugs
Feb. 16	HUMAN RIGHTS: Economic and Social Council established Commission on Human Rights
Feb. 16	EMPLOYMENT: Economic and Social Council established Economic and Employment Commission
Feb. 16	SOCIAL: Economic and Social Council established Temporary Social Commission
Feb. 16	STATISTICS: Economic and Social Council established Statistical Commission
Feb. 16	TRANSPORT & COMMUNICATIONS: Economic and Social Council established Temporary Transport and Communication Commission
Feb. 16	SYRIA-LEBANON: (1st veto-U.S.S.R.): Security Council recommendation to the parties
March 21	HEADQUARTERS: temporary headquarters established at Hunter College, New York City
April 3	COURT: 1st meeting of the International Court of Justice
April 8	SPAIN: situation brought to the Security Council by Poland
April 8 - 18	LEAGUE OF NATIONS: dissolved
May 25 - June 21	ECONOMIC AND SOCIAL COUNCIL: 2nd session
June 14	ATOMIC ENERGY: International atomic development authority proposed to U.N. Atomic Energy Commission by U.S. (Baruch plan)
June 19	ATOMIC ENERGY: Convention to outlaw production and use of atomic weapons proposed to U.N. Atomic Energy Commission by U.S.S.R.
June 19 - July 22	HEALTH: constitution for World Health Organization drafted by U.N. International Health Conference
June 21	FREEDOM OF INFORMATION: Subcommission on Freedom of Information authorized by Economic and Social Council
June 18	SPAIN: (2nd veto-U.S.S.R.): Security Council endorsement of certain principles
	SPAIN: (3rd veto-U.S.S.R.): Security Council recommendation to the General Assembly
	SPAIN: (4th veto-U.S.S.R.): Security Council recommendation to the Secretary-General
	SPAIN: (5th veto U.S.S.R.): Security Council resolution containing substance of matters under vetoes 2-4.
June 21	WOMEN: Commission on the Status of Women established by the Economic and Social Council
June 21	DEVASTATED AREAS: Subcommission on Devastated Areas established by Economic and Social Council
June 21	NON-GOVERNMENTAL ORGANIZATIONS: consultative status established by Economic and Social Council
June 24	MEMBERSHIP: Mongolian People's Republic applied
June 26	SPAIN: (6th veto-U.S.S.R. and France): Security Council proposal for simultaneous discussion by the General Assembly
June 26	SPAIN: (7th veto-U.S.S.R.): retention of item on Security Council agenda

1946 (Continued)

July 2	MEMBERSHIP: Afghanistan applied
July 8	MEMBERSHIP: Jordan applied
July 29 - Sept. 13	RECONSTRUCTION: 1st session of the Temporary Subcommission on the Economic Reconstruction of Devastated Areas
Aug. 1	LEAGUE OF NATIONS: property and assets transferred to the U.N.
Aug. 2	MEMBERSHIP: Iceland, Ireland and Portugal applied
Aug. 5	MEMBERSHIP: Thailand applied
Aug. 9	MEMBERSHIP: Sweden applied
Aug. 16 - 19	HEADQUARTERS: moved to Lake Success
Aug. 24	GREECE: situation created by Balkan policy of Greek Government brought to Security Council by the Ukraine
Aug. 29	MEMBERSHIP: (8th to 10th vetoes-U.S.S.R.): Security Council voting on applications of Jordan, Ireland and Portugal.
Sept. 11 - Oct. 3	ECONOMIC AND SOCIAL COUNCIL: 3rd session
Sept. 20	GREECE: (11th veto-U.S.S.R.): Security Council establishment of commission of investigation
Sept. 21	SPECIALIZED AGENCIES: establishment of Administrative Committee on Co-ordination (ACC)
Sept. 26	ATOMIC ENERGY: Scientific and Technical Committee of the Atomic Energy Commission reported no scientific evidence that effective control was not possible
Oct. 1	FISCAL: Economic and Social Council established Fiscal Commission
Oct. 3	POPULATION: Economic and Social Council established Population Commission
Oct. 23 - Dec. 15	GENERAL ASSEMBLY: 1st session, second part
Nov. 19	MEMBERSHIP: Afghanistan, Iceland and Sweden admitted as 52nd, 53rd and 54th Members
Nov. 19	NARCOTIC DRUGS: transfer of League of Nations functions approved by General Assembly
Nov. 27 - Dec. 13	NARCOTIC DRUGS: 1st session of Commission on Narcotic Drugs
Dec. 3	GREECE: situation on borders brought to Security Council by Greece
Dec. 8	UNION OF SOUTH AFRICA: recommendation to the parties by the General Assembly concerning Indians in the Union of South Africa
Dec. 11	CHILRREN: U.N. International Children's Emergency Fund (UNICEF) established by the General Assembly
Dec. 11	INTERNATIONAL LAW: principles of Nurnberg approved by the General Assembly
Dec. 12	SPAIN: debarment from specialized agencies approved by General Assembly
Dec. 14	NON-SELF-GOVERNING TERRITORIES: Ad Hoc Committee on Information from Non-Self-Governing Territories established by General Assembly
Dec. 13	TRUSTEESHIP: agreements for New Guinea, Ruanda-Urundi, British and French Togoland, British and French Cameroons, Tanganyika and Western Samoa approved by the General Assembly
Dec. 14	ARMS CONTROL: General Assembly asked Security Council to take steps to bring about a reduction

1946 (Continued)

Dec. 14	HEADQUARTERS: New York selected as permanent headquarters by General Assembly, which also accepted $8,500,000 gift from J. D. Rockefeller, Jr.
Dec. 14	BUDGET: $47,130,000 authorized—$19,390,000 for 1946 and $27,740,000 for 1947
Dec. 14	SOCIAL: General Assembly decided to continue the social welfare work of the U.N. Relief and Rehabilitation Administration
Dec. 14	SPECIALIZED AGENCIES: General Assembly approved agreements with the International Labour Organization (ILO), the U.N. Food and Agriculture Organization (FAO), the U.N. Educational, Scientific and Cultural Organization (UNESCO) and the International Civil Aviation Organization (ICAO)
Dec. 14	SOUTHWEST AFRICA: General Assembly rejected incorporation by Union of South Africa
Dec. 15	REFUGEES: constitution of International Refugee Organization approved by the General Assembly
Dec. 15	MEMBERSHIP: Thailand admitted as 55th Member
Dec. 19	GREECE: Commission of Investigation (Balkans Commission) established by the Security Council
Dec. 31	ATOMIC ENERGY: 1st report of U.N. Atomic Energy Commission recommended in international system of inspection and control.

1947

Jan. 10	CORFU CHANNEL CASE: damage to ships brought to Security Council by U.K.
Jan. 10	TRIESTE: Security Council accepts responsibility
Jan. 20 - Feb. 4	SOCIAL: 1st session of Social Commission
Jan. 20 - Feb. 5	ECONOMIC: 1st session of Economic and Employment Commission
Jan. 27 - Feb. 10	HUMAN RIGHTS: 1st session of Commission on Human Rights
Jan. 27 - Feb. 7	STATISTICS: 1st session of Statistical Commission
Feb. 4 - 18	SOCIAL WELFARE: 1st session of Temporary Social Welfare Committee
Feb. 6 - 18	TRANSPORT AND COMMUNICATION: 1st session of Transport and Communications Commission
Feb. 6 - 19	POPULATION: 1st session of Population Commission
Feb. 10 - 24	WOMEN: 1st session of Commission on the Status of Women
Feb. 10	FREEDOM OF INFORMATION: Subcommission on Freedom of Information and of the Press established by Human Rights Commission
Feb. 10	MINORITIES: Subcommission on Prevention of Discrimination and Protection of Minorities established by Human Rights Commission
Feb. 13	ARMS CONTROL: Commission for Conventional Armaments established by Security Council
Feb. 28 - March 29	ECONOMIC AND SOCIAL COUNCIL: 4th session
March 25	CORFU CHANNEL: (12th veto-U.S.S.R.): Security Council recommendation to the parties
March 26 - April 28	TRUSTEESHIP COUNCIL: 1st session
March 28	ECONOMIC COMMISSION FOR EUROPE: established by Economic and Social Council

13

1947 (Continued)

March 28	ECONOMIC COMMISSION FOR ASIA AND THE FAR EAST: established by the Economic and Social Council
April 2	PALESTINE: Special Session of the General Assembly proposed by the U.K.
April 2	TRUSTEESHIP: trusteeship agreement for the Trust Territory of the Pacific Islands approved by the Security Council
April 9	CORFU CHANNEL: referal to the International Court of Justice recommended by the Security Council
April 22	MEMBERSHIP: Hungary applied
April 24	TRUSTEESHIP: lrst visiting mission approved by Trusteeship Council—to Western Samoa
April 28 - May 15	GENERAL ASSEMBLY: 1st special session—Palestine
April 30	ARMS CONTROL: Military Staff Committee report on general principles re Article 43
May 2 - 14	ECONOMIC COMMISSION FOR EUROPE: 1st session
May 7	MEMBERSHIP: Italy applied
May 12 - June 17	INTERNATIONAL LAW: 1st session of the Committee on the Progressive Development of International Law and its Codification
May 15	PALESTINE: Special Committee on Palestine (UNSCOP) established by General Assembly
May 19 - 29	FISCAL COMMISSION: 1st session
May 19 - June 4	FREEDOM OF INFORMATION: 1st session of Subcommission on Freedom of Information and of the Press
June 16 - 25	ECONOMIC COMMISSION FOR ASIA AND THE FAR EAST (ECAFE): 1st session
June 25	GREECE: report of the Commission of Investigation (Balkans Commission)
June 26	HEADQUARTERS: agreement between U.S. and Secretary-General signed
July 2	MEMBERSHIP: Austria applied
July 8	EGYPT: presence of British troops brought to Security Council
July 10	MEMBERSHIP: Romania applied
July 19 - Aug. 17	ECONOMIC AND SOCIAL COUNCIL: 5th session
July 24 - Aug. 8	NARCOTIC DRUGS: 1st session of Commission on Narcotic Drugs
July 26	MEMBERSHIP: Bulgaria applied
July 29	GREECE: (13th veto-U.S.S.R.): investigation commission proposed by Security Council
July 30	INDONESIA: situation brought to Security Council by Australia and India
Aug. 1	INDONESIA: cease fire between Dutch and Indonesians called for by Security Council
Aug. 8	CHILDREN: U.N. Appeal for Children approved by Economic and Social Council
Aug. 15	MEMBERSHIP: Pakistan applied
Aug. 18	MEMBERSHIP: (14th, 15th & 16th vetoes-U.S.S.R.): applications of Jordan, Ireland and Portugal
Aug. 19	GREECE: (17th veto-U.S.S.R.): determination of a threat to the peace
Aug. 19	MEMBERSHIP: (18th veto-U.S.S.R.): states to cease aid to guerillas
Aug. 21	MEMBERSHIP: (19th-20th vetoes: U.S.S.R.): Security Council voting on applications of Italy and Austria

1947 (Continued)

Aug. 25	INDONESIA: (21st veto-France and U.S.S.R.): establishment of a commission of investigation by the Security Council
Aug. 25	INDONESIA: Good Offices Committee set up by the Security Council
Aug. 31	PALESTINE: partition recommended by UNSCOP
Sept. 8 - 12:	STATISTICS: World Statistical Congress
Sept. 11	ATOMIC ENERGY: report by U.N. Atomic Enery Commission on principles to govern an international agency
Sept. 15	GREECE: (22nd veto-U.S.S.R.): proposal for consideration by the General Assembly
Sept. 19	MEMBERSHIP: Finland applied
Sept. 24	TRIESTE: (23rd veto presumed-U.S.S.R.): nomination of a governor—private meeting.
Sept. 16 - Nov. 29	GENERAL ASSEMBLY: 2nd session
Sept. 30	MEMBERSHIP: Pakistan and Yemen admitted as 56th and 57th members
Oct. 1	MEMBERSHIP: (24th and 25th vetoes-U.S.S.R.): applications of Italy and Finland
Oct. 20	FLAG: General Assembly adopted U.N. Flag
Oct. 21	GREECE: establishment of Special Committee on the Balkans (UNSCOB) by the General Assembly
Oct. 30	TRADE: Protocol of Provisional Application of General Agreements on Tariff and Trade (GATT) signed
Nov. 1	SOUTHWEST AFRICA: General Assembly again recommended that territory be placed under trusteeship
Nov. 1	TRUSTEESHIP: General Assembly approved trusteeship for Nauru
Nov. 13	INTERIM COMMITTEE OF THE GENERAL ASSEMBLY established
Nov. 14	KOREA: General Assembly established Temporary Commission on Korea (UNTCOK)
Nov. 15	SPECIALIZED AGENCIES: General Assembly approved agreements bringing into relationship with the U.N. the International Bank for Reconstruction and Development (IBRD), the International Monetary Fund (IMF), the Universal Postal Union (UPU), and the International Telecommunication Union (ITU)
Nov. 17	EDUCATION: General Assembly recommends that Members encourage teaching about the U.N. in schools
Nov. 20	HEADQUARTERS: General Assembly approved design and $65 million loan from U.S. for permanent building
Nov. 20	BUDGET: $35,671,763 authorized—$846,568 for 1947 and $34,825,195 for 1948
Nov. 20 - Dec. 16	TRUSTEESHIP COUNCIL: second session, first part
Nov. 21	INTERNATIONAL LAW COMMISSION: established by the General Assembly
Nov. 21 - March 24	TRADE: Conference on Trade and Employment to draw up charter for an International Trade Organization (ITO) Havana
Nov. 29	PALESTINE: partition plan approved by General Assembly: Jerusalem to be under an international regime
Dec. 8	TRUSTEESHIP: first personal appearance of a petitioner from a trust territory before a principal organ of the United Nations—Sylvanus E. Olympio from French Togoland before the Trusteeship Council

1948

Jan. 17	INDONESIA: Renville agreement signed by Netherlands and Indonesia
Jan. 20	KASHMIR: U.N. Commission for India-Pakistan established by Security Council
Feb. 2 - March 11	ECONOMIC AND SOCIAL COUNCIL: 6th session
Feb. 18 - March 10	TRUSTEESHIP COUNCIL: 2nd part of 2nd session
Feb. 19 - March 6	TRANSPORT: U.N. Maritime Conference drafted convention for an Inter-governmental Maritime Consultative Organization (IMCO)
Feb. 25	ECONOMIC COMMISSION FOR LATIN AMERICA (ECLA): established by Economic and Sodial Council
March 5	PALESTINE: Security Council appealed to all Governments to prevent disorders
March 23	HEADQUARTERS: $65,000,000 loan agreement with United States
March 23 - April 21	FREEDOM OF INFORMATION: three conventions adopted by U.N. Conference on Freedom of Information
March 24	TRADE: Charter of an International Trade Organization signed (Havana)
March 30	ATOMIC ENERGY: Committee 2 (Control) of U.N. Atomic Energy Commission adjourned because of stalemate
April 1	PALESTINE: Security Council called for special session of General Assembly
April 10	MEMBERSHIP: (26th veto-U.S.S.R.): Security Council voting on application of Italy
April 16	PALESTINE: Security Council called for cessation of hostilities
April 16 - May 14	GENERAL ASSEMBLY: 2nd special session
April 19	MEMBERSHIP: Burma admitted as 58th Member
April 21 - May 5	TRUSTEESHIP COUNCIL: 3rd part of 2nd session
April 21	KASHMIR: plebiscite recommended by Security Council
April 23	PALESTINE: Truce Commission established by Security Council
May 10	KOREA: elections in South Korea observed by UNTCOK
May 14	PALESTINE: termination of the Mandate
May 14	PALESTINE: Mediator for Palestine established by General Assembly
May 14	ISRAEL: proclaimed an independent state and recognized by U.S.
May 15	PALESTINE: Egypt announced entrance of Egyptian troops into Palestine
May 20	PALESTINE: Count Folke Bernadotte appointed Mediator
May 22	PALESTINE: Security Council called upon all states to abstain from hostile military actions
May 24	CZECHOSLOVAKIA: (27th veto-U.S.S.R.): establishment of an investigation commission
May 28	MEMBERSHIP: advisory opinion of International Court of Justice
May 29	PALESTINE: Security Council refused to order Governments to cease military operations, as proposed by U.S.S.R. with support of U.S.: called upon Governments to cease-fire
June 11	PALESTINE: truce agreement accepted by all parties
June 15	PALESTINE: U.S.S.R. proposal for military observers from Permanent Members rejected by Security Council
June 16 - Aug. 5	TRUSTEESHIP COUNCIL: 3rd session

1948 (Continued)

June 22	ATOMIC ENERGY: (28th veto-U.S.S.R.): report of the U.N. Atomic Energy Commission
June 25	KOREA: UNTCOK resolved that elections in South Korea expressed free will of people
July 6	TRUSTEESHIP: first regular visiting mission constituted—Tanganyika and Ruanda-Urundi
July 15	PALESTINE: Security Council ordered a cease fire
July 19 - Aug. 29	ECONOMIC AND SOCIAL COUNCIL: 7th session
July 28	INTERNATIONAL COURT OF JUSTICE: Switzerland became a part to the Statute
Aug. 13	KASHMIR: cease-fire called for by Security Council
Aug. 18	MEMBERSHIP: (29th veto-U.S.S.R.): Security Council voting on application of Ceylon
Sept. 17	PALESTINE: Count Bernadotte assassinated
Sept. 21 - Dec. 12	GENERAL ASSEMBLY: 1st part of 3rd session
Oct. 1	CHILDREN: announcement that U.N. Appeal for Children had received $18,000,000
Oct. 2	ATOMIC ENERGY: U.S.S.R. proposed that there be separate conventions on prohibition and control
Oct. 8	NARCOTIC DRUGS: protocol on synthetic drugs
Oct. 25	BERLIN: (30th veto-U.S.S.R.): recommendation to the parties
Nov. 4	ATOMIC ENERGY: international control and production approved by General Assembly
Nov. 18	TRUSTEESIIP: increased educational facilities recommended by General Assembly
Nov. 18	SPECIALIZED AGENCIES: agreement with IRO approved by General Assembly
Nov. 19	PALESTINE: U.N. Relief for Palestine Refugees (UNRPR) established by General Assembly—$25,000,000 voluntary contributions envisaged
Nov. 26	SOUTHWEST AFRICA: General Assembly again recommended that the territory be placed under trusteeship
Nov. 27	GREECE: return of all Greek children asked by General Assembly
Dec. 3	WOMEN: CHILDREN: OBSCENE PUBLICATIONS: functions exercised by French Government in connection with traffic in women, children and obscene publications transferred to U.N.
Dec. 4	TECHNICAL ASSISTANCE: Secretary-General authorized to provide certain types of assistance to Governments
Dec. 9	GENOCIDE: Convention approved by General Assembly
Dec. 10	HUMAN RIGHTS: Universal Declaration adopted by General Assembly
Dec. 11	BUDGET: $47,947,669 authorized—$4,469,541 for 1948 and $43,487,128 for 1949
Dec. 11	PALESTINE: Conciliation Commission established by General Assembly
Dec. 12	KOREA: General Assembly endorsed Government of the Republic of Korea and established U.N. Commission on Korea (UNCOK)
Dec. 15	MEMBERSHIP: (31st veto-U.S.S.R.): Security Council voting on application of Ceylon
Dec. 24	INDONESIA: Security Council called for cease-fire
Jan. 1	KASHMIR: cease-fire ordered by India and Pakistan

1949

Jan. 24 - March 25	TRUSTEESHIP COUNCIL: fourth session
Jan. 28	INDONESIA: cease-fire ordered by Security Council; program of action set forth calling, *inter alia* for transfer of sovereignty to Indonesia
Feb. 7 - March 18	ECONOMIC AND SOCIAL COUNCIL: eighth session
Feb. 24	PALESTINE: Egypt-Israel armistice
March 21	KASHMIR: Chester W. Nimitz named by Security Council as Plebiscite Administrator
March 23	PALESTINE: Lebanon-Israel armistice
April 3	PALESTINE: Jordan-Israel armistice
April 5 May 18	GENERAL ASSEMBLY: second part of third session
April 8	MEMBERSHIP: (32nd veto-U.S.S.R.): application of Republic of Korea
April 9	CORFU CHANNEL CASE: International Court of Justice ruled that Albania was responsible for damage to British ships
April 11	LEGAL PERSONALITY OF THE U.N.: International Court of Justice rendered advisory opinion that U.N. had the capacity to bring an international claim against a government
April 14	SECURITY COUNCIL VOTING: General Assembly recommended list of 34 items that should not be subject to veto
April 28	PACIFIC SETTLEMENT OF DISPUTES: General Assembly set up Panel for Inquiry and Conciliation
May 4	BERLIN BLOCKADE: agreement of four powers to lift the blockade on May 12
May 7	INDONESIA: preliminary agreement between Netherlands and Indonesia
May 11	MEMBERSHIP: Israel admitted as 59th Member
May 12	BERLIN: blockade lifted
May 14	INDIANS IN UNION OF SOUTH AFRICA: General Assembly invited parties to hold a round-table conference
June 15 - July 22	TRUSTEESHIP COUNCIL: 5th session
July 5 - Aug. 15	ECONOMIC AND SOCIAL COUNCIL: 9th session
July 11	SOUTHWEST AFRICA: cessation of reporting announced by Union of South Africa
July 20	PALESTINE: Syria-Israel armistice agreement
July 29	ATOMIC ENERGY: U.N. Atomic Energy Commission suspended work
Aug. 11	PALESTINE: Security Council terminated office of Acting Mediator
Aug. 15	TECHNICAL ASSISTANCE: expanded program recommended by Economic and Social Council
Aug. 17 - Sept. 6	CONSERVATION: U.N. Scientific Conference on the Conservation and Utilization of Resources
Aug. 23 - Sept. 19	TRANSPORT: U.N. Conference on Road and Motor Transport
Aug. 23 - Nov. 2	INDONESIA: Round Table Conference adopted Charter on transfer of sovereignty
Sept. 7	MEMBERSHIP: (33rd veto-U.S.S.R.): Security Council voting on application of Nepal
Sept. 13	MEMBERSHIP: (34th to 40th vetoes-U.S.S.R.) Security Council voting on applications of Portugal, Jordan, Italy, Finland, Ireland, Austria and Ceylon
Sept. 20 - Dec. 10	GENERAL ASSEMBLY: 4th session

1949 (Continued)

Sept. 27	TRUSTEESHIP COUNCIL: 1st special session
Oct. 11	ARMS CONTROL: (41st veto-U.S.S.R.): Report of Commission on Conventional Armaments
Oct. 18	ARMS CONTROL: (42nd veto-U.S.S.R.): verification of armaments
Oct. 18	ARMS CONTROL: (43rd veto-U.S.S.R.): regulation of armaments
Oct. 21	KOREA: General Assembly continues the U.N. Commission on Korea (UNCOK)
Oct. 22	BULGARIA, HUNGARY AND ROMANIA: General Assembly requests advisory opinion from the International Court of Justice
Oct. 22 - Dec. 16	EMPLOYMENT: meeting of five experts on measures for full employment
Nov. 15	TRUSTEESHIP: General Assembly adopts seven resolutions concerning welfare of inhabitants
Nov. 16	TECHNICAL ASSISTANCE: General Assembly approved expanded programme
Nov. 17	SOCIAL WELFARE: General Assembly placed advisory services on a permanent basis
Nov. 18	GREECE: General Assembly instructed Secretary-General to seek assistance from Red Cross agencies in aiding return of Greek children
Nov. 21	LIBYA: General Assembly decided on independence by January 1, 1952
Nov. 21	SOMALILAND: General Assembly decided on independence after ten years of Italian administration as a trust territory
Nov. 21	ERITREA: General Assembly established Commission to ascertain the wishes of the people
Nov. 22	PANEL OF FIELD OBSERVERS: General Assembly authorized the Secretary-General to maintain a list of persons qualified to supervise truces and observe plebiscites
Nov. 22	U.N. FIELD SERVICE: authorized by General Assembly
Nov. 23	ATOMIC ENERGY: control plan approved by General Assembly
Nov. 24	U.N. ADMINISTRATIVE TRIBUNAL: established by General Assembly
Dec. 1	LEGAL PERSONALITY OF THE U.N.: General Assembly authorized Secretary-General to bring reparations claims against Members or non-members
Dec. 1	PEACEFUL SETTLEMENT: "Essentials of Peace" resolution adopted by the General Assembly
Dec. 2	TRAFFIC IN PERSONS: Convention for the Suppression of the Traffic in Persons and of the Exploitation of the Prostitution of Others adopted by the General Assembly
Dec. 3	REFUGEES: Office of the High Commissioner for Refugees established by the General Assembly
Dec. 6	SOUTHWEST AFRICA: General Assembly again recommended that territory be placed under trusteeship; urged renewal of reporting by the Union of South Africa; and requested an advisory opinion from the International Court of Justice
Dec. 8	PALESTINE: U.N. Relief and Works Agency for Palestine Refugees in the Near East (UNRWAPRNE) established by General Assembly

1949 (Continued)

Dec. 8 - 20	TRUSTEESHIP COUNCIL: 2nd Special session
Dec. 9	ADMINISTRATIVE TRIBUNAL: members appointed
Dec. 9	PALESTINE: internationalization of Jerusalem again approved by General Assembly
Dec. 10	BUDGET: $49,358,725 authorized for 1950
Dec. 10	LIBYA: U.N. Commissioner appointed by General Assembly
Dec. 13	INDONESIA: (44th veto-U.S.S.R.): composition of a commission of investigation
Dec. 13	INDONESIA: (45th veto-U.S.S.R.): congratulations to the parties
Dec. 15	CORFU CHANNEL: International Court of Justice fixed $2,-400,000 compensation to be paid by Albania
Dec. 27	INDONESIA: Netherlands transferred sovereignty over whole territory except New Guinea (West Irian)

1950

Jan. 13	CHINA: U.S.S.R. withdrew from Security Council on issue of Chinese representation
Jan. 19 - April 4	TRUSTEESHIP COUNCIL: 6th session
Feb. 7 - March 6	ECONOMIC AND SOCIAL COUNCIL: 10th session
Feb. 27	NON-GOVERNMENTAL ORGANIZATIONS: status clarified by Economic and Social Council
March 1	FIELD SERVICE: established by Secretary-General
March 3	MEMBERSHIP: International Court of Justice advisory opinion that admission requires a recommendation from the Security Council
March 3	EGYPT-FRANCE CASE: decision by International Court of Justice
March 14	KASHMIR: Security Council liquidated Commission for India-Pakistan and called for demilitarization within five months
March 15 - April 6	MISSING PERSONS: U.N. Conference on Declaration of Death of Missing Persons
March 29	INTERNATIONAL COURT OF JUSTICE: Liechtenstein became a party to the Statute
March 30	BULGARIA, HUNGARY AND RUMANIA: International Court of Justice advisory opinion on peace treaties
April 12	KASHMIR: Sir Owen Dixon appointed U.N. Representative for India-Pakistan by the Security Council
June 1 - July 21	TRUSTEESHIP COUNCIL: 7th session
June 6	SECRETARY-GENERAL: Trygve Lie's Twenty Year Peace Plan circulated
June 12 - 14	TECHNICAL ASSISTANCE: 1st Pledging Conference — $20,070,260 for eighteen months to December 1951
June 14	PALESTINE: Israel paid reparations for assassination of Count Bernadotte
June 25	KOREA: Security called upon North Korea to withdraw to 37th parallel, upon Members to refrain from giving assistance to North Korea, and upon Members to give every assistance to the U.N. in carrying out this resolution. (U.S.S.R. absent)
June 27	KOREA: Security Council called upon Members to furnish assistance to the Republic of Korea
July 3 - Aug. 16	ECONOMIC AND SOCIAL COUNCIL—11th session (Geneva)

1950 (Continued)

July 11	SOUTHWEST AFRICA: International Court of Justice Advisory Opinion that there was not an obligation to place the territory under trusteeship, but that the Union of South Africa could not unilaterally determine the future of the territory
July 17	KOREA: Security Council established unified U.N. Command
July 18	BULGARIA, HUNGARY AND RUMANIA: International Court of Justice Advisory opinion that Secretary-General not authorized to appoint a commissioner when parties had not done so
July 31	KOREA: Security Council requested U.N. Command to determine relief requirements
Aug. 1	U.S.S.R.: returned to Security Council
Aug. 9	FREEDOM OF INFORMATION: Committee to draft a convention appointed by General Assembly
Aug. 21	HEADQUARTERS: first units of Secretariat move into permanent buildings in New York
Sept. 6	KOREA: (46th veto-U.S.S.R.): determination of a breach of the peace
Sept. 12	CHINA BOMBING: (47th veto-U.S.S.R.): establishment of a commission of investigation
Sept. 15	KASHMIR: U.N. Representative reported inability to secure agreement on demilitarization
Sept. 16	SUEZ: Israel complaint to Security Council that Egypt had maintained a blockade of the canal
Sept. 19 - May 18, 1951	GENERAL ASSEMBLY: 5th session (officially the session lasted until November 5, 1951)
Sept. 28	MEMBERSHIP: Indonesia admitted as 60th Member
Oct. 7	KOREA: U.N. Commission for the Unification and Rehabilitation of Korea (UNCURK) established by the General Assembly
Oct. 12 - Dec. 13	ECONOMIC AND SOCIAL COUNCIL: 2nd part of 11th session
Oct. 12	SECRETARY-GENERAL: (48th veto-U.S.S.R.): re-appointment of Trygve Lie
Oct. 25 - Nov. 21	COMMODITIES: U.N. Tin Conference (Geneva)
Nov. 3	UNITING FOR PEACE: resolution adopted by General Assembly
Nov. 3	PEACE OBSERVATION GROUP: established by General Assembly
Nov. 4	SPAIN: two 1946 resolutions revoked by General Assembly
Nov. 5	KOREA: presence of Chinese communist troops reported by U.N. Command
Nov. 8	CHINA: Peoples Republic invited to send a representative to the Security Council
Nov. 16	POSTAL ADMINISTRATION: U.N. Postal Administration established by the General Assembly
Nov. 17	PALESTINE: Security Council called upon Egypt, Jordan and Israel to settle their complaints
Nov. 17	DUTIES OF STATES: General Assembly recommended procedure to be followed by states in event of hostilities
Nov. 20	TWENTY YEAR PEACE PROGRAM: Secretary-General commended by General Assembly
Nov. 20	ASYLUM CASE: judgment by International Court of Justice
Nov. 22	TRUSTEESHIP COUNCIL: 3rd Special Session

1950 (Continued)

Nov. 27	ASYLUM CASE: interpretation by International Court of Justice—Nov. 20 judgment.
Nov. 30	KOREA: (49th veto-U.S.S.R.): proposal for provisional measures
Dec. 1	GREECE: General Assembly called for repatriation of members of Greek armed forces; established Standing Committee
Dec. 1	CHILDREN: UNICEF continued for three years and emphasis changed from relief to continuing aid
Dec. 1	SOCIAL WELFARE: General Assembly expanded program
Dec. 1	KOREA: General Assembly established U.N. Korean Relief and Reconstruction Agency (UNKRA)
Dec. 2	INDIANS IN SOUTH AFRICA: General Assembly recommended a committee to assist the parties and a round-table discussion
Dec. 2	UNION OF SOUTH AFRICA: General Assembly called upon the Union to refrain from implementing Group Areas Act (apartheid)
Dec. 2	SOMALILAND: General Assembly approved trusteeship agreement with Italy
Dec. 2	ERITREA: General Assembly recommended federation with Ethiopia
Dec. 4	HUMAN RIGHTS: General Assembly decided to include economic, social and cultural rights in one covenant
Dec. 12	KOREA: General Assembly authorized service ribbons
Dec. 13	SOUTHWEST AFRICA: General Assembly established committee of five to confer with the Union of South Africa and to consider reports and petitions
Dec. 14	KOREA: General Assembly established four-man group to determine basis of a cease-fire
Dec. 14	PALESTINE: General Assembly expressed concern for refugees and directed Conciliation Commission to establish office for assessment and payment of compensation
Dec. 14	PRISONERS: General Assembly established Ad Hoc Commission on Prisoners of War
Dec. 14	REFUGEES: General Assembly adopted Statute of the Office of the High Commissioner for Refugees and elected G. J. van Heuven Goodhart
Dec. 15	BUDGET: $42,677,000 authorized for 1951
Dec. 15	LIBYA: General Assembly established U.N. Tribunal to assist in determining boundaries
Dec. 15	SOMALILAND: procedure for determining boundaries determined by General Assembly
Dec. 15	PALESTINE: General Assembly unable to agree on a resolution on the status of Jerusalem
Dec. 23	KOREA: People's Republic of China declared Cease Fire Group illegal and refused participation

1951

Jan. 1	REFUGEES: High Commissioner's Office came into being
Jan. 12	GENOCIDE: Convention came into force
Jan. 30 - March 16	TRUSTEESHIP COUNCIL: 8th session

1951 (Continued)

Feb. 1	KOREA: People's Republic of China declared an aggressor by the General Assembly; Good Offices Committee and Additional Measures Committee established
Feb. 13	CHINA: General Assembly rejected U.S.S.R. charges of U.S. aggression
Feb. 19 - May 2	ECONOMIC DEVELOPMENT: Committee of Experts recommended establishment of an International Finance Corporation (IFC) and an international development authority
Feb. 20 - March 21	ECONOMIC AND SOCIAL COUNCIL: 12th session
March 5 - Oct. 3	COLLECTIVE MEASURES COMMITTEE: meetings
March 14	INDONESIA: U.N. Commission for Indonesia decided military observers no longer needed
March 19	FORCED LABOUR: Ad Hoc committee established by Economic and Social Council
March 28	POSTAL ADMINISTRATION: agreement with U.S. whereby U.N. issued and used its own stamps
March 29	LIBYA: provisional government established
March 30	KASHMIR: Frank P. Graham appointed U.N. Representative by Security Council
April 3	INDONESIA: U.N. Commission adjourned
May 8	PALESTINE: Israel instructed by Security Council to cease work in Huleh marshes
May 18	KOREA: embargo against North Korea and People's Republic of China recommended by General Assembly
May 18	PALESTINE: Armistice Agreement machinery strengthened by Security Council
May 28	GENOCIDE: effect of reservations to Convention given in advisory opinion by International Court of Justice
June 5 - July 30	TRUSTEESHIP COUNCIL: 9th session
June 13	ASYLUM CASE: judgment by International Court of Justice
June 29	KOREA: U.N. Command offered to discuss cease-fire
July 1	KOREA: Communist commander proposed cease-fire discussions take place near Kaesong
July 2 - 25	REFUGEES: U.N. Conference on the Status of Refugees and Stateless Persons
July 5	IRAN: provisional measures in Anglo-Iranian Oil Company case indicated by International Court of Justice
July 10	KOREA: cease-fire talks begin
July 16	KOREA: agreement on relationship between U.N. Command and UNKRA
July 25	REFUGEES: Convention Relating to the Status of Refugees signed
July 25	TRAFFIC IN PERSONS: Convention came into force
July 30 - Sept. 21	ECONOMIC AND SOCIAL COUNCIL: 1st part of 13th session
Aug. 1 - 31	CRIMINAL JURISDICTION: 1st session of U.N. Committee on International Criminal Jurisdiction
Sept. 1	SUEZ: termination of Egyptian restrictions on shipping called for by Security Council
Sept. 18	ECONOMIC AND EMPLOYMENT COMMISSION: terminated
Oct. 24	POSTAL ADMINISTRATION: 1st U.N. stamps issued
Nov. 5	TECHNICAL ASSISTANCE: 1st major project for training in public administration (Rio de Janeiro)
Nov. 5	GENERAL ASSEMBLY: 5th session ended

1951 (Continued)

Nov. 6 - Feb. 5	GENERAL ASSEMBLY: 6th session
Nov. 10	KASHMIR: U.N. Representative instructed by Security Council to continue efforts to secure agreement on demilitarization
Nov. 13	CHINA: question of representation in General Assembly postponed by vote of 37 to 11, with 4 abstentions
Nov. 27	KOREA: provisional truce
Dec. 14	YUGOSLAVIA: General Assembly recommended that Communist governments conduct their relations with Yugoslavia in the spirit of the Charter
Dec. 18 - 20	ECONOMIC AND SOCIAL COUNCIL: 2nd part of 13th session
Dec. 18	TRUSTEESHIP COUNCIL: 4th special session
Dec. 18	ANGLO-NORWEGIAN FISHERIES CASE: judgment by International Court of Justice
Dec. 20	GERMANY: Commission to ascertain possibility of free elections appointed by General Assembly
Dec. 20	SPECIALIZED AGENCIES: agreement with World Meteorological Organization (WMO) approved by General Assembly
Dec. 21	BUDGET: $54,748,650 authorized—$1,126,900 for 1951 and $53,621,780 for 1952 ($5,524,970 not authorized until February 4, 1952)
Dec. 24	LIBYA: became independent and applied for Membership

1952

Jan. 11	ARMS CONTROL: Disarmament Commission to replace Atomic Energy Commission and Commission on Conventional Armaments established by General Assembly
Jan. 12	ECONOMIC DEVELOPMENT: General Assembly requested Economic and Social Council to prepare a plan for a fund for economic development (later to be called SUNFED)
Jan. 18	TRUSTEESHIP: abolition of corporal punishment recommended by General Assembly; Members invited to provide scholarships
Jan. 19	SOUTHWEST AFRICA: Ad Hoc Committee established by General Assembly
Jan. 23	PEACE OBSERVATION COMMISSION: established Balkans Sub-commission
Jan. 24	MISSING PERSONS: Convention came into force
Jan. 26	PALESTINE: UNRAWAPRNE $50 million program for relief and $200 million program for rehabilitation endorsed by General Assembly
Jan. 31	KASHMIR: U.N. Representative asked by Security Council to continue efforts for peaceful settlement
Jan. 31	REFUGEES: IRO terminated operations
Jan. 31	GREECE: military observers for Greek frontiers decided upon by Balkans Sub-commission of Peace Observation Commission
Feb. 5	HUMAN RIGHTS: General Assembly decided to have two conventions, an article on self-determination and study of effects of reservations to covenants
Feb. 6	MEMBERSHIP: (50th veto-U.S.S.R.): Security Council voting on application of Italy

1952 (Continued)

Feb. 6 - 7	TECHNICAL ASSISTANCE: 2nd Pledging Conference — $18,795,355
Feb. 27	HEADQUARTERS: new building in New York formally inaugurated
Feb. 27 - April 1	TRUSTEESHIP COUNCIL: 10th session
March 3 - 21	FREEDOM OF INFORMATION: final session of Sub-commission
March 4	ECONOMIC AND SOCIAL COUNCIL: 1st special session
March 26	TRANSPORT: Convention on Road Traffic came into force
April 5	ARMS CONTROL: U.S. proposal to Disarmament Commission for disclosure and verification
April 14	TUNISIA: agenda item rejected by Security Council
May 20 - Aug. 1	ECONOMIC AND SOCIAL COUNCIL: 14th session
May 28	ARMS CONTROL: numerical limitation proposed to Disarmament Commission by France, U.K. and U.S.
June 3 - July 24	TRUSTEESHIP COUNCIL: 1st part of 11th session
June 20	TUNISIA: request for Special Session of General Assembly rejected—only 23 Members approved
June 23	ECONOMIC DEVELOPMENT: committee to prepare plan for Special United Nations Fund for Economic Development (SUNFED) appointed by Economic and Social Council
July 1	AMBATIELOS CASE: judgment by International Court of Justice
July 3	BACTERIOLOGICAL WARFARE: (51st veto-U.S.S.R.): proposal for establishment of a commission of investigation
July 9	BACTERIOLOGICAL WARFARE: (52nd veto-U.S.S.R.): impartial investigation
July 22	IRAN: International Court of Justice denied its own jurisdiction in Anglo-Iranian Oil Co. case
Aug. 5	GERMANY: U.N. Commission to Investigate Conditions for Free Elections in Germany adjourned because of inability to establish contact with authorities in Soviet zone
Aug. 27	U.S. CITIZENS IN MOROCCO CASE: judgment of International Court of Justice
Sept. 11	ERITREA: federated with Ethiopia
Sept. 16	MEMBERSHIP: (53rd veto-U.S.S.R.): Security Council voting on application of Libya
Sept. 18	MEMBERSHIP: (54th veto-U.S.S.R.): Security Council voting on application of Japan
Sept. 19	MEMBERSHIP: (55th to 57th vetoes-U.S.S.R.): Security Council voting on applications of Viet Nam, Laos and Cambodia
Oct. 1	MISSING PERSONS: opening of International Bureau for the Declaration of Death of Missing Persons
Oct. 14 - Dec. 22	GENERAL ASSEMBLY: 1st part of 7th session
Oct. 25	CHINA: question of representation in General Assembly postponed by vote of 42 to 7, with 11 abstentions
Nov. 1	HYDROGEN BOMB: 1st test by U.S.
Nov. 6	PALESTINE: $23,000,000 budget for UNRWPARNE authorized for year ending June 30, 1953
Nov. 10	SECRETARY-GENERAL: Trygve Lie submitted resignation
Nov. 19 - Dec. 3	TRUSTEESHIP COUNCIL: 2nd part of 13th session
Dec. 3	KOREA: Repatriation Commission proposed by General Assembly to facilitate return of prisoners

1952 (Continued)

Dec. 5	UNION OF SOUTH AFRICA: Commission on the Racial Situation in the Union of South Africa established by the General Assembly
Dec. 10	NON-SELF-GOVERNING TERRITORIES: Ad Hoc Committee on Factors established by General Assembly
Dec. 16 - 19	ECONOMIC AND SOCIAL COUNCIL: resumed 14th session
Dec. 16	FREEDOM OF INFORMATION: Convention on the International Right of Correction opened by the General Assembly for signature
Dec. 21	TRUSTEESHIP: greater participation of inhabitants in work of Trusteeship Council approved by the General Assembly
Dec. 17	GREECE: failure of neighboring states, except Yugoslavia, to repatriate Greek children condemned by General Assembly
Dec. 17	TUNISIA: confidence in negotiations of parties expressed by General Assembly
Dec. 19	MOROCCO: confidence in negotiations of parties expressed by General Assembly
Dec. 20	WOMEN: Convention on Political Rights of Women approved by General Assembly
Dec. 21	BUDGET: $50,778,580 authorized—$2,450,880 for 1952 and $48,327,700 for 1953
Dec. 22	KOREA: mass murder of prisoners charged by U.S.S.R. rejected by General Assembly
Dec. 23	KASHMIR: India and Pakistan urged by Security Council to negotiate with U.N. Representative

1953

Feb. 24 - April 23	GENERAL ASSEMBLY: 2nd part of 7th session
Feb. 26 - 27	TECHNICAL ASSISTANCE: 3rd Pledging Conference — $22,395,687
March 13	SECRETARY-GENERAL: (58th veto-U.S.S.R.): nomination of Lester Pearson
March 23	KASHMIR: Report of U.N. Representative not discussed
March 31 - Apr. 28	ECONOMIC AND SOCIAL COUNCIL: 15th session
April 8	ARMS CONTROL: General Assembly called upon Disarmament Commission to continue its work
April 10	SECRETARY-GENERAL: appointment of Dag Hammarskjold
April 11	KOREA: agreement on exchange of sick and wounded prisoners
April 23	ECONOMIC DEVELOPMENT: report of committee proposing creation of SUNFED.
April 23	BURMA: presence of foreign troops condemned by General Assembly
April 23	BACTERIOLOGICAL WARFARE: General Assembly established Commission to investigate charges
May 11 - June 18	NARCOTIC DRUGS: protocol to limit trade in and use of opium adopted by U.N. Opium Conference
May 20	AMBATIELOS CASE: judgment by International Court of Justice
June 8	KOREA: agreement on prisoners of war
June 16 - July 21	TRUSTEESHIP COUNCIL: 12th session
June 30 - Aug. 5	ECONOMIC AND SOCIAL COUNCIL: 16th session

1953 (Continued)

July 27	KOREA: armistice agreement created Neutral Nations Supervisory Commission and Neutral Nations Repatriation Commission (NNSC and NNRC)
July 27 - Aug. 20	CRIMINAL JURISDICTION: statute for an International Criminal Court drafted by Committee on International Criminal Jurisdiction
July 30	KOREA: withdrawal of U.N. troops from demilitarized zone
Aug. 5 - Sept. 6	KOREA: exchange of prisoners in "Operation Big Switch"
Aug. 17 - 28	GENERAL ASSEMBLY: resumed 7th session
Aug. 28	KOREA: conference to be held not later than October 28th recommended by General Assembly
Sept. 10	KOREA: Neutral Nations Repatriation Commission began to assume custody of prisoners
Sept. 15 - Dec. 9	GENERAL ASSEMBLY: 1st part of 8th session
Sept. 15	CHINA: question of representation in General Assembly postponed by veto of 44 to 10, with 2 abstentions
Sept. 24	KOREA: 21,601 prisoners transferred by U.N. Command: 359 by Communist command
Oct. 6	CHILDREN: U.N. Children's Fund placed on permanent basis by General Assembly, with retention of symbol "UNICEF"
Oct. 23	SLAVERY: transfer to U.N. of League of Nations functions under Slavery Convention of 1926
Oct. 27	PALESTINE: suspension of work on diversion of Jordan River water by Israel approved by Security Council
Nov. 11	TUNISIA: General Assembly unable to agree on a resolution
Nov. 12 - 13	TECHNICAL ASSISTANCE: 4th Pledging Conference — $24,000,000: U.S.S.R. participated for first time
Nov. 17	MINQUIERS-ECREHOS ISLANDS: judgment by International Court of Justice
Nov. 18	NOTTEBOHM CASE: preliminary judgment by International Court of Justice
Nov. 24	PALESTINE: Israel censured by Security Council for action at Qibya
Nov. 27	PALESTINE: UNRWAPRNE budget of $24.8 million for year ending June 30, 1954 and $18 million for relief during year ending June 30, 1955 authorized by General Assembly.
Nov. 27	NON-SELF-GOVERNING TERRITORIES: list of factors adopted by General Assembly
Nov. 27	PUERTO-RICO: cessation of transmission of information by U.S. approved by General Assembly
Nov. 28	SOUTHWEST AFRICA: General Assembly reiterated that territory should be placed under trusteeship
Nov. 28	HUMAN RIGHTS: federal clause and right of petition considered by General Assembly
Nov. 28	ARMS CONTROL: establishment of sub-commission of powers principally concerned suggested to Disarmament Commission by General Assembly
Nov. 30 - Dec. 7	ECONOMIC AND SOCIAL COUNCIL: resumed 16th session
Dec. 3	KOREA: concern over treatment of U.N. prisoners expressed by General Assembly
Dec. 7	FORCED LABOR: Economic and Social Council and ILO invited by General Assembly to consider report of Ad Hoc Committee on Forced Labor

1953 (Continued)

Dec. 7	PRISONERS OF WAR: states holding World War II prisoners called upon by General Assembly to provide an opportunity for repatriation
Dec. 7	KOREA: UNKRA program to July 1, 1955 approved by General Assembly
Dec. 7	ECONOMIC DEVELOPMENT: Raymond Scheyven appointed by General Assembly to examine replies of Governments concerning Special United Nations Fund for Economic Development (SUNFED)
Dec. 8	ATOMIC ENERGY: International Atomic Energy Agency proposed by President of the U.S. to the General Assembly
Dec. 8	UNION OF SOUTH AFRICA: General Assembly expressed concern at report of Commission on Racial Situation in the Union of South Africa
Dec. 8	BURMA: efforts to evacuate foreign troops approved by General Assembly
Dec. 9	BUDGET: $49,368,860 authorized—$1,541,750 for 1953 and $47,827,110 for 1954
Dec. 20	TRANSPORT: Protocol on Road Signs and Signals came into force

1954

Jan. 10	GENERAL ASSEMBLY: Indian proposal for reconvened 8th session rejected—only 22 Members approved
Jan. 22	PALESTINE: (59th veto-U.S.S.R.): call upon Syria and Israel to co-operate on diversion of waters of River Jordan
Jan. 23	KOREA: all remaining prisoners released by Neutral Nations Repatriation Commission
Jan. 28 - March 25	TRUSTEESHIP COUNCIL: 13th session
Feb. 18	INTERNATIONAL COURT OF JUSTICE: San Marino became a party to the Statute
March 29	SUEZ: (60th veto-U.S.S.R.): call upon Egypt to comply with 1951 resolution of Security Council on restrictions on shipping
March 30 - Apr. 30	ECONOMIC AND SOCIAL COUNCIL: 17th session
April 2	INTERNATIONAL COURT OF JUSTICE: Japan became a party to the Statute
April 9-19	ARMS CONTROL: meetings of Disarmament Commission
April 22	REFUGEES: Convention on Status of Refugees came into force
April 26 - June 15	KOREA: Foreign Ministers fail to agree on peaceful unification
May 11 - June 4	TRANSPORT: U.N. Conference on Customs Formalities for the Temporary Importation of Road Meter Vehicles and for Tourism adopted two conventions
May 13	ECONOMIC DEVELOPMENT: 1st Scheyven report on SUNFED
May 13 - July 22	ARMS CONTROL: Subcommission of Disarmament Commission meetings
June 2 - July 16	TRUSTEESHIP COUNCIL: 14th session
June 15	ALBANIAN GOLD: International Court of Justice rendered decision
June 18	THAILAND: (61st veto-U.S.S.R.): request to Security Council for Peace Observation Commission observers

1954 (Continued)

June 20	GUATEMALA: Security Council called for termination of action likely to lead to bloodshed: (62nd veto-U.S.S.R.) referral to Organization of American States
June 29 - Aug. 6	ECONOMIC AND SOCIAL COUNCIL: 18th session
July 7	WOMEN: Convention on the Political Rights of Women came into force
July 12	HUNGARY vs. U.S. CASE: International Court of Justice found that Hungary and U.S.S.R. refused jurisdiction of the Court
July 13	ADMINISTRATIVE TRIBUNAL AWARDS: International Court of Justice rendered advisory opinion
July 20 - 29	ARMS CONTROL: Disarmament Commission meetings
Aug. 1	GREECE: military observers discontinued by Balkans Sub-commission of Peace Observation Commission
Aug. 5	FISCAL: termination of Fiscal Commission by Economic and Social Council
Aug. 5	COMMODITIES: establishment of Commission on International Commodity Trade by Economic and Social Council
Aug. 10	ECONOMIC DEVELOPMENT: 2nd Scheyven report on SUNFED
Aug. 31 - Sept. 10	POPULATION: meeting of U.N. World Population Conference
Sept. 13 - 24	STATELESSNESS: convention approved by U.N. Conference of Plenipotentiaries on the Status of Stateless Persons
Sept. 20	GENERAL ASSEMBLY: 8th session reconvened
Sept. 21 - Dec. 17	GENERAL ASSEMBLY: 9th session
Sept. 21	CHINA: question of representation in General Assembly postponed by veto of 45 to 7, with 5 abstentions
Oct. 11	SOUTHWEST AFRICA: General Assembly adopted rules concerning reports, petitions and voting
Oct. 21	REFUGEES: five year $12 million plan of High Commissioner approved by General Assembly
Oct. 29	BURMA: disarmament and internment of foreign troops approved by General Assembly
Nov. 23	SOUTHWEST AFRICA: three resolutions adopted by General Assembly, including a request for an advisory opinion from the International Court of Justice on the applicability of the two-thirds voting rule in the General Assembly
Nov. 26	TECHNICAL ASSISTANCE: 5th Pledging Conference — $27,965,550 by 60 nations
Nov. 26	TECHNICAL ASSISTANCE: measures for co-ordination of national and international agencies approved by General Assembly
Dec. 4	ATOMIC ENERGY: draft statute of IAEA approved by General Assembly
Dec. 4	HUMAN RIGHTS: comments on two draft covenants sought by General Assembly from Governments and specialized agencies
Dec. 10	KOREA: Secretary-General requested by General Assembly to assist in securing release of prisoners
Dec. 10	WEST IRIAN (NEW GUINEA): General Assembly unable to agree on a resolution
Dec. 11	ECONOMIC DEVELOPMENT: Raymond Scheyven's appointment extended for one year to give further study to replies of Governments concerning SUNFED

1954 (Continued)

Dec. 11	INTERNATIONAL FINANCE CORPORATION: International Bank for Reconstruction and Development asked by General Assembly to prepare draft statute
Dec. 17	BUDGET: $50,665,670 authorized; $701,870 for 1954 and $49,963,800 for 1955
Dec. 17	TUNISIA: confidence in negotiations of parties expressed by General Assembly

1955

Jan. 5 - 10	KOREA: Secretary-General in Peiping negotiating for release of prisoners
Jan. 25 - March 28	TRUSTEESHIP COUNCIL: 15th session
Feb. 3	CHINA: People's Republic declines Security Council invitation to participate in discussion of offshore islands
Feb. 15 - 25	CARTOGRAPHY: U.N. Regional Cartography Conference for Asia and the Far East
Feb. 25 - May 18	ARMS CONTROL: meetings of Sub-committee of Disarmament Commission
March 7	TRADE: Organization for Trade Co-operation (OTC) proposed by GATT
March 7 - 25	ECONOMIC DEVELOPMENT: meeting of Scheyven Committee to discuss SUNFED
March 29 - April 7	ECONOMIC AND SOCIAL COUNCIL: 19th session
March 29	PALESTINE: Security Council condemned attack by Israeli armed forces in Gaza
April 6	NOTTEBOHM CASE: judgment rendered by International Court of Justice
April 15	INTERNATIONAL FINANCE CORPORATION: charter proposed by International Bank for Reconstruction and Development
May 9	ARMS CONTROL: comprehensive proposal submitted to Subcommittee of Disarmaments Commission by U.S.S.R.
May 16 - 27	ECONOMIC AND SOCIAL COUNCIL: resumed 19th session
June 1	ARMS CONTROL: meeting of Subcommittee of Disarmament Commission
June 7	SOUTHWEST AFRICA: advisory opinion rendered by International Court of Justice
June 8 - July 22	TRUSTEESHIP COUNCIL: 16th session
June 20 - 26	COMMEMORATION OF TENTH ANNIVERSARY OF CHARTER
July 1	ARMS CONTROL: aerial photographs proposal by U.S.
July 5 - Aug. 5	ECONOMIC AND SOCIAL COUNCIL: 20th session
July 23	ARMS CONTROL: "Summit" meeting of heads of states referred questions to Subcommittee of Disarmament Commission
Aug. 4	KOREA: eleven prisoners released by Communists
Aug. 8 - 20	ATOMIC ENERGY: first International Conference on the Peaceful Uses of Atomic Energy
Aug. 29 - Oct. 7	ARMS CONTROL: meetings of Subcommittee of Disarmament Subcommission
Sept. 8	PALESTINE: Security Council called on Egypt and Israel to co-operate with U.N. Chief of Staff
Sept. 13	ARMS CONTROL: U.K. proposed to Subcommittee of Disarmament Commission a plan for control test area in Europe
Sept. 20 - Dec. 20	GENERAL ASSEMBLY: 10th session

1955 (Continued)

Sept. 20	CHINA: question of representation in General Assembly postponed by vote of 42 to 12, with 5 abstentions
Sept. 23	CYPRUS: agenda item rejected by General Assembly
Sept. 30	ALGERIA: contrary to recommendation of General Committee, item placed on agenda of General Assembly
Oct. 3 - 17	COMMODITIES: U.N. Conference on Olive Oil
Oct. 21	ARMS CONTROL: meeting of Disarmament Commission
Oct. 24 - Dec. 14	TRUSTEESHIP COUNCIL: 5th special session
Oct. 26 - Nov. 16	COMMODITIES: U.N. Wheat Conference
Oct. 26	TECHNICAL ASSISTANCE: 6th Pledging Conference — $28,964,563 by 72 Governments
Nov. 2	PALESTINE: Secretary-General's appeal to the parties
Nov. 3	INTERNATIONAL FINANCE CORPORATION: statute approved by General Assembly
Nov. 21	CHARTER: committee to consider time and place for review conference established by General Assembly
Nov. 23	ARMS CONTROL: meeting of Disarmament Commission
Nov. 25	ALGERIA: General Assembly decided not to consider further
Dec. 2	HUMAN RIGHTS: General Assembly completed tentative approval of preambles and common article 1 of both Covenants
Dec. 3	MOROCCO: General Assembly hoped for successful negotiations between parties
Dec. 3	SOUTHWEST AFRICA: General Assembly adopted nine resolutions; reiterated that territory should be under trusteeship; requested advisory opinion from International Court of Justice as to right to hear oral petitions; informed petitioners that territory was still under mandate
Dec. 3	RADIATION: U.N. Scientific Committee on the Effects of Atomic Radiation established by General Assembly
Dec. 3	ATOMIC ENERGY: continued the Advisory Committee On Peaceful uses
Dec. 5 - 15	ECONOMIC AND SOCIAL COUNCIL: resumed 20th session
Dec. 9	ECONOMIC DEVELOPMENT: General Assembly submitted eight questions re SUNFED to Governments and established committee of sixteen to examine replies
Dec. 13	MEMBERSHIP: (63rd veto-China): Security Council voting on application of Outer Mongolia
	MEMBERSHIP: (64th to 78th vetoes—U.S.S.R.): Security Council voting on applications of Republic of Korea, Viet Nam, Jordan, Ireland, Portugal, Italy, Austria, Finland, Ceylon, Nepal, Libya, Cambodia, Japan, Laos and Spain
Dec. 14	MEMBERSHIP: (79th veto-U.S.S.R.): Security Council voting on application of Japan
	MEMBERSHIP: Albania, Jordan, Ireland, Portugal, Hungary, Italy, Austria, Romania, Bulgaria, Finland, Ceylon, Nepal, Libya, Cambodia, Laos and Spain admitted as 61st to 76th Members
Dec. 15	TRUSTEESHIP: Commissioner for British Togoland election elected by General Assembly
Dec. 15	MEMBERSHIP: (80th veto-U.S.S.R.): Security Council voting on application of Japan
Dec. 15	GERMANY: Federal Republic admitted to Economic Commission for Europe

1955 (Continued)

Dec. 15   NON-SELF-GOVERNING TERRITORIES: cessation of transmission of information from Netherlands Antilles and Surinam approved by General Assembly

Dec. 16   BUDGET: $51,830,550 authorized — $3,264,200 for 1955 and $48,566,350 for 1956

Dec. 16   TRUSTEESHIP: General Assembly recommended consultation with inhabitants of French Togoland, under U.N. supervision

Dec. 16   CHARTER: Security Council concurred in establishment of Committee on Review Conference established by General Assembly on November 21

Dec. 19   WEST IRIAN (NEW GUINEA): General Assembly hoped for fruitful negotiations between parties

Dec. 22   INDIA: right of passage case brought to the International Court of Justice by Portugal

Dec. 31   KOREA: contributions to UNKRA total $139,835,101 out of $226,000,000 target

1956

Feb. 7 - April 6   TRUSTEESHIP COUNCIL: 17th session

March 14   AERIAL INCIDENT CASE: International Court of Justice ordered U.S. vs. Czechoslovakia case removed from list

March 14   AERIAL INCIDENT CASE: International Court of Justice ordered U.S. vs. U.S.S.R. case removed from list

March 16   ANTARCTICA CASE: International Court of Justice ordered U.K. vs. Chile case removed from list

March 16   ANTARCTICA CASE: International Court of Justice ordered U.K. vs. Argentina case removed from list

March 19 - May 4   ARMS CONTROL: Subcommittee of Disarmament Commission met

April 9   RADIATION: first report of U.N. Scientific Committee on the Effects of Atomic Radiation

April 17   PALESTINE: Secretary-General arrived in Middle East

April 17 - May 4   ECONOMIC AND SOCIAL COUNCIL: 21st session

April 18   ATOMIC ENERGY: draft statute of International Atomic Energy Agency approved by drafting committee

May 9   TRUSTEESHIP: British Togoland plebiscite on union with Gold Coast (Ghana) supervised by U.N. Commissioner

June 1   SOUTHWEST AFRICA: advisory opinion on petitions rendered by International Court of Justice

June 7 - Aug. 14   TRUSTEESHIP COUNCIL: 18th session

June 26   ALGERIA: agenda item rejected by Security Council

July 3 - 16   ARMS CONTROL: Disarmament Commission met

July 9 - Aug. 9   ECONOMIC AND SOCIAL COUNCIL: 22nd session

July 24   INTERNATIONAL FINANCE CORPORATION: began operation

Sept. 7   SLAVERY: Convention on the Abolition of Slavery, Slave Trade, and Institutions and Practices similar to Slavery signed by 33 states

Sept. 20 - Oct. 26   ATOMIC ENERGY: Statute of International Atomic Energy Agency signed by 70 states

Oct. 17   TECHNICAL ASSISTANCE: 7th Pledging Conference — $30,874,133 for 1957

Oct. 13   PALESTINE: (81st veto-U.S.S.R.): Security Council call upon Egypt to cease certain practices

1956 (Continued)

Oct. 13	SUEZ: Security Council adopted six principles for settlement of Suez question
Oct. 23	TRUSTEESHIP: plebiscite in French Togoland
Oct. 28	HUNGARY: situation placed on agenda of Security Council
Oct. 29	SUEZ: Israeli invasion of Egypt
Oct. 30	SUEZ: (82nd veto-U.K. and France): Security Council call upon U.K. and France to refrain from use of force
Oct. 30	SUEZ: (83rd veto-U.K. and France): Security Council call upon Israel to refrain from use of force
Oct. 31	SUEZ: French-U.K. attack
Nov. 1 - 10	GENERAL ASSEMBLY: 1st Emergency Special Session (Suez)
Nov. 2	SUEZ: General Assembly urged cease fire and withdrawal of all forces and that steps be taken to re-open Suez Canal
Nov. 4	HUNGARY: (84th veto-U.S.S.R.): Security Council call upon U.S.S.R. to desist from use of force
Nov. 4 - 10	GENERAL ASSEMBLY: 2nd Emergency Session (Hungary)
Nov. 4	SUEZ: General Assembly requested Secretary-General to submit a plan for a U.N. Emergency Force: later on same day plan was submitted (UNEF)
Nov. 5	U.N. EMERGENCY FORCE: established by General Assembly
Nov. 7	SUEZ: Israel, France and U.K. requested by General Assembly to withdraw forces
Nov. 8	SUEZ: first salvage firms to clear Canal appointed by Secretary-General
Nov. 10	UNEF: 1st contingents arrived in Italy
Nov. 12	UNEF: Egypt agreed to establishment of UNEF on Egyptian territory
Nov. 12 - March 8	GENERAL ASSEMBLY: 11th session
Nov. 12	MEMBERSHIP: Sudan, Morocco and Tunisia admitted as 77th to 79th Members
Nov. 15	UNEF: first contingents arrive in Ismailia
Nov. 16	SUEZ: Secretary-General arrived in Egypt
Nov. 16	CHINA: question of representation in General Assembly postponed by vote of 47 to 24, with 9 abstentions
Nov. 18	SUEZ: Egypt requested U.N. assistance in clearing Canal
Nov. 20	SUEZ: aide-memoire on terms of Secretary-General's agreement with Egypt on UNEF
Nov. 21	SUEZ: General Assembly agreed to apportion first $10 million of cost of UNEF according to regular assessment formula
Nov. 24	SUEZ: R. A. Wheeler and John J. McCloy appointed to assist and advise on Canal clearance
Nov. 24	SUEZ: General Assembly regretted failure of Israeli, French and British troops to withdraw
Dec. 10 - Jan. 31	TRUSTEESHIP COUNCIL: 6th Special Session
Dec. 13 - 26	HUMAN RIGHTS: General Assembly tentatively approved article 6-12 of Covenant on Economic, Social and Cultural Rights
Dec. 18	MEMBERSHIP: Japan admitted as 80th Member
Dec. 21	BUDGET: $62,932,700 authorized: $2,117,000 for 1956, $48,-807,650 for 1957 and $10,000,000 for UNEF. (a further $2,008,050 on February 27, 1957)
Dec. 22	SUEZ: Anglo-French withdrawal completed
Dec. 28	SUEZ: clearance of Canal began

1957

Jan. 23	SOUTHWEST AFRICA: General Assembly authorized Committee to hear petitioners
Jan. 24	KASHMIR: Security Council reiterated decision for free plebiscite
Jan. 30	UNION OF SOUTH AFRICA: Apartheid deplored by General Assembly
Jan. 30	INDIANS IN UNION OF SOUTH AFRICA: General Assembly urged parties to negotiate
Feb. 2	SUEZ: General Assembly called upon Israel to withdraw
Feb. 14	ARMS CONTROL: General Assembly recommended that Disarmament Commission consider several proposals
Feb. 15	ALGERIA: General Assembly hoped for peaceful settlement
Feb. 20	INTERNATIONAL FINANCE CORPORATION: General Assembly approved agreement bringing IFC into relationship with Economic and Social Council
Feb. 20	KASHMIR: (85th veto-U.S.S.R.): Security Council consideration of possible use of a U.N. force
Feb. 20	KASHMIR: Security Council requested Gunnar Jarring to seek a solution
Feb. 20	WOMEN: Convention on the Nationality of Married Women approved by General Assembly
Feb. 26	ECONOMIC DEVELOPMENT: General Assembly requested Ad Hoc Committee to make suggestions
Feb. 26	CYPRUS: General Assembly hoped for resumption of negotiations
Feb. 26	SOUTHWEST AFRICA: General Assembly adopted seven resolutions, including request to Committee to study what legal courses of action were open
Feb. 28	WEST IRIAN (NEW GUINEA): General Assembly unable to agree on a resolution
March 8	MEMBERSHIP: Ghana admitted as 81st Member
March 14 - May 15	TRUSTEESHIP COUNCIL: 19th session
March 18 - Sept. 6	ARMS CONTROL: meetings of Subcommittee of Disarmament Commission
April 8 - 18	RADIATION: Meetings of Scientific Committee
April 16 - May 2	ECONOMIC AND SOCIAL COUNCIL: 23rd session
April 16	TRUSTEESHIP: French decree promulgating Statute for the Cameroons
April 29	KASHMIR: Jarring reported that he was unable to suggest concrete proposals likely to contribute to a solution
May 20 - July 12	TRUSTEESHIP COUNCIL: 20th session
July 2 - Aug. 2	ECONOMIC AND SOCIAL COUNCIL: 24th session
July 6	NORWAY-FRANCE CASE: International Court of Justice declined jurisdiction
July 29	ATOMIC ENERGY: IAEA came into being
Aug. 2	NON-SELF-GOVERNING TERRITORIES: Belgium announced that information would be transmitted to U.N. Library
Sept. 9	MEMBERSHIP: (86th veto-U.S.S.R.): Security Council voting on admission of Republic of Korea
Sept. 9	MEMBERSHIP: (87th veto-U.S.S.R.): Security Council voting on admission of Viet Nam
Sept. 10 - 14	GENERAL ASSEMBLY: resumed 11th session
Sept. 12 - 20	TRUSTEESHIP COUNCIL: 7th special session

1957 (Continued)

Sept. 17 - Dec. 14	GENERAL ASSEMBLY: 12th session
Sept. 17	MEMBERSHIP: Malaya admitted as 82nd Member
Sept. 24	CHINA: question of representation in General Assembly postponed by vote of 47 to 27, with 7 abstentions
Oct. 2	INTERHANDEL CASE: SWITZERLAND VS. UNITED STATES: brought to International Court of Justice
Oct. 10	TECHNICAL ASSISTANCE: 8th Pledging Conference — $32,317,900
Oct. 10	NETHERLANDS-SWEDEN CASE: brought to International Court of Justice
Oct. 11 - Nov. 4	HUMAN RIGHTS: General Assembly tentatively approved Articles 14-16 of Covenant on Economic-Social and Cultural Rights
Oct. 16	AERIAL INCIDENT CASE: ISRAEL, UNITED KINGDOM AND UNITED STATES vs. BULGARIA: case brought to International Court of Justice
Oct. 25	SOUTHWEST AFRICA: Good Offices Committee established by General Assembly
Nov. 13 - 25	HUMAN RIGHTS: General Assembly tentatively approved Article 6 of Covenant on Civil and Political Rights
Nov. 14	RADIATION: General Assembly called upon all concerned to co-operate with Scientific Committee
Nov. 19	ARMS CONTROL: membership of Disarmament Commission increased from 11 to 25
Nov. 26	UNION OF SOUTH AFRICA: failure to change racial policies deplored by General Assembly
Nov. 26	NON-SELF-GOVERNING TERRITORIES: proposal for study of Charter interpretations rejected by General Assembly
Nov. 26	TRADE: Members urged by General Assembly to approve establishment of OTC
Nov. 26	KOREA: termination of UNKRA on June 30, 1958 approved by General Assembly
Nov. 26	REFUGEES: Office of High Commission continued by General Assembly for 5 years
Nov. 26	REFUGEES: General Assembly appealed for activities for Hong Kong refugees
Nov. 27	BELGIUM vs. NETHERLANDS CASE: border problem brought to International Court of Justice
Nov. 29	WEST IRIAN: General Assembly unable to agree on a resolution
Nov. 29	KOREA: General Assembly reiterated objective of peaceful unification
Dec. 2	KASHMIR: Security Council requested U.N. Representative to make recommendations
Dec. 9	HUNGARY: Special Representative reported that his negotiations with the U.S.S.R. and Hungary had been fruitless
Dec. 10	ALGERIA: General Assembly wished that parties would enter into pourparlers
Dec. 10 - 13	ECONOMIC AND SOCIAL COUNCIL: resumed 24th session
Dec. 14	REGIONAL OFFICES: land in Santiago, Chile accepted by General Assembly
Dec. 14	ECONOMIC DEVELOPMENT: General Assembly decided to establish Special Fund for technical assistance instead of SUNFED

1957 (Continued)

Dec. 14	BUDGET: $87,421,850 authorized—$2,359,000 for 1957 and $55,062,850 for 1958; and $30,000,000 for UNEF.
Dec. 14	CYPRUS: General Assembly unable to agree on a resolution
Dec. 14	TRUSTEESHIP: General Assembly recommended establishment of an Arbitration Tribunal in connection with Ethiopian boundary
Dec. 14	TRUSTEESHIP: General Assembly elected Commissioner to supervise French Togoland elections
Dec. 14	SUEZ: three percent surcharge on Canal tolls approved by General Assembly to pay for $8,400,000 cost of clearing the Canal
Dec. 16	PALESTINE: Secretary-General named Francisco Uurrutia Holquin as his personal representative to Jordan and Israel
Dec. 21	HUNGARY: permanent representative of Hungary refused to transmit to his Government letter from Special Committee on the Problem of Hungary
Dec. 31	CHILDREN: UNICEF contributions totalled $17,899,811 for 1957

1958

Jan. 18	PALESTINE: agreement on Mt. Scopus situation by Israel and Jordan reported by Secretary-General's representative
Jan. 22	PALESTINE: suspension of incidents in Jerusalem called for by Security Council
Jan. 27 - Feb. 28	RADIATION: meetings of Scientific Committee
Jan. 30 - March 26	TRUSTEESHIP COUNCIL: 21st session
Feb. 18	TUNISIA: complaint of French air attack on Sakiet-Sidi-Youssef heard by Security Council; UK-US offer of good offices
Feb. 22	SUDAN: complaint against Egyptian boundary claims heard by Security Council
Feb. 24 - April 27	INTERNATIONAL LAW: final act, four conventions and a protocol approved by U.N. Conference on the Law of the Sea
Feb. 26 - 27	NON-GOVERNMENTAL ORGANIZATIONS: Conference on U.N. Information
March 6	UNITED ARAB REPUBLIC (UAR): membership of U.N. reduced to 81 as credentials of permanent representative of the U.A.R. comprising Egypt and Syria, presented to the Secretary-General
March 11 - Apr. 15	TECHNICAL ASSISTANCE: meeting of the Preparatory Committee of the Special Fund
March 17	TRANSPORT: IMCO agreement came into effect with acceptance by Japan
March 31	HEADQUARTERS: 4 millionth visitor
March 31	KASHMIR: five recommendations to parties reported to Security Council by U.N. Representative
April 15 - May 2	ECONOMIC AND SOCIAL COUNCIL: 25th session
April 21	ARMS CONTROL: U.S.S.R. complaint of U.S. flights in the Arctic heard by the Security Council
April 27	TRUSTEESHIP: elections in French Togoland supervised by U.N. Commissioner
April 29	AFRICA: Economic Commission for Africa established by Economic and Social Council

1958 (Continued)

April 30	REFUGEES: Executive Committee of the Program of the High Commissioner for Refugees established by the Economic and Social Council
April 30	ATOMIC TESTING: unilateral discontinuance of testing announced to U.N. by the U.S.S.R.
May 2	ARMS CONTROL: (88th veto-U.S.S.R.): plan for an Arctic inspection zone
May 7-8	ATOMIC ENERGY: meeting of Advisory Committee on Peaceful Uses of Atomic Energy
May 22	LEBANON: complaint to Security Council of U.A.R. intervention in domestic affairs of Lebanon
June 4	TUNISIA: Security Council adjourned debate until June 18th to permit parties to negotiate
June 9 - Aug. 1	TRUSTEESHIP COUNCIL: 22nd session
June 10	INTERNATIONAL LAW: Convention on the Recognition and Enforcement of Foreign Arbitral Awards adopted by U.N. Conference on International Commercial Arbitration
June 11	LEBANON: United Nations Observer Group in Lebanon (UNOGIL) established by Security Council
June 18	TUNISIA: agreement for evacuation of French troops notified to Security Council
June 21	HUNGARY: Special Committee on the Problem of Hungary deplored executions of Imre Nagy, Pal Maleter and others
June 30	BUDGET: available cash balances of U.N. adequate for only three weeks operations
July 1	HONDURAS-NICARAGUA CASE: case brought to International Court of Justice by Honduras
July 1 - 31	ECONOMIC AND SOCIAL COUNCIL: 26th session
July 14	IRAQ: coup resulting in change of Government
July 14	HUNGARY: report of Special Committee on Problem of Hungary
July 15	LEBANON: Security Council notified of landing of U.S. troops
July 16	LEBANON: UNOGIL reported full freedom of access to borders of Lebanon
July 17	JORDAN: complaint to Security Council of U.A.R. interference in domestic affairs of Jordan
July 18	LEBANON: Security Council defeated U.S.S.R. proposal for withdrawal of UK and U.S. forces from Jordan and Lebanon; defeated Swedish proposal for suspension of UNOGIL: (89th veto-U.S.S.R.): U.S. proposal for additional measures in Lebanon
July 19	MIDDLE EAST: Secretary-General invited by U.S.S.R. to summit conference on Middle East
July 21	LEBANON: (90th veto-U.S.S.R.): Japanese proposal to strengthen UNOGIL
Aug. 8 - 21	GENERAL ASSEMBLY: 3rd Emergency Special Session—on Middle East—called by Security Council on Aug. 7
Aug. 10	RADIATION: first comprehensive report by Scientific Committee on the Effects of Atomic Radiation
Aug. 11	WOMEN: Convention on Nationality of Married Women came into effect
Aug. 13	MIDDLE EAST: six point peace program proposed by President of the U.S. to General Assembly

1958 (Continued)

Aug. 21	LEBANON-JORDAN: General Assembly called upon all states to act in accordance with mutual respect and requested Secretary-General to make practical arrangements
Aug. 21	ARMS CONTROL: eight Powers agree that a workable and effective system for detecting explosions is feasible
Aug. 22	AERIAL INCIDENT CASE: U.S. brought case against U.S.S.R. to the International Court of Justice
Aug. 26	LEBANON: UNOGIL reported 190 military observers from fifteen countries
Sept. 1 - 12	ATOMIC ENERGY: second U.N. International Conference on the Peaceful Uses of Atomic Energy
Sept. 8 - 10	COMMODITIES: U.N. Exploratory Meeting on Copper
Sept. 11 - 13	COMMODITIES: U.N. Exploratory Meeting on Lead
Sept. 15	TRUSTEESHIP COUNCIL: 8th special session
Sept. 16 - Dec. 13	GENERAL ASSEMBLY: 13th session
Sept. 20	LEBANON: UNOGIL reported 214 military observers from 21 countries
Sept. 22	COMMODITIES: U.N. Sugar Conference
Sept. 23	CHINA: question of representation in the General Assembly postponed by vote of 42 to 28, with eleven abstentions
Sept. 23	BARCELONA LIGHT & POWER CO. CASE: brought to International Court of Justice by Belgium
Sept. 29	LEBANON-JORDAN: Secretary-General reported on practical measures, including U.N. "presence" in the area
Oct. 13 - 17	TRUSTEESHIP COUNCIL: 8th special session
Oct. 13	TRUSTEESHIP: France informed the Trusteeship Council that French Togoland would become independent in 1960
Oct. 16 - 29	HUMAN RIGHTS: General Assembly tentatively adopted articles 7 - 9 of the Craft Covenant on Civil and Political Rights
Oct. 16	TECHNICAL ASSISTANCE: 9th pleging Conference—$27,-000,000 for the Expanded Program and $21,000,000 for the Special Fund
Oct. 23 - Dec. 11	ECONOMIC AND SOCIAL COUNCIL: resumed 26th session
Oct. 25	LEBANON: U.S. troops withdrawn
Oct. 27	PALESTINE: $27.5 million pledged by 32 governments for UNRWA
Oct. 27	REFUGEES: $3.1 million pledged by 26 governments for Office of the High Commissioner for Refugees programmes
Oct. 30	SOUTHWEST AFRICA: General Assembly rejected partition
Oct. 30	UNION OF SOUTH AFRICA: General Assembly regretted no change in apartheid policy
Nov. 2	JORDAN: U.K. troops withdrawn
Nov. 4	ARMS CONTROL: early agreement on testing urged by General Assembly
Nov. 4	ARMS CONTROL: early agreement on measures against surprise attack urged by General Assembly
Nov. 4	ARMS CONTROL: membership of Disarmament Commission increased from 25 to 81—all Members of U.N.
Nov. 6 - 7	TRUSTEESHIP COUNCIL: 9th special session
Nov. 14	KOREA: General Assembly called on Communist authorities to agree to free elections
Nov. 14	HUMAN RIGHTS: General Assembly tentatively adopted text of article 10 of the Draft Covenant on Civil and Political Rights

1958 (Continued)

Dec. 4	TECHNICAL ASSISTANCE: Paul G. Hoffman appointed Managing Director of U.N. Special Fund
Dec. 5	TRUSTEESHIP: Trusteeship Council asked to report to resumed session of the General Assembly on February 20, 1959 concerning the possibility of independence for both Cameroons
Dec. 5	TRUSTEESHIP: General Assembly invited administering authorities to consider target dates for self-government of trust territories
Dec. 5	CYPRUS: General Assembly expressed confidence that parties would reach a solution
Dec. 5	REFUGEES: General Assembly urged Members to co-operate in a Refugee Year
Dec. 8	PALESTINE: Security Council heard Israeli complaint against U.A.R. attack
Dec. 9	LEBANON: UNOGIL ceased operations
Dec. 10	INTERNATIONAL LAW: General |Assembly decided to convene a second International Conference on the Law of the Sea in 1960
Dec. 10	LIBYA: General Assembly invited governments to give economic assistance
Dec. 12	HUNGARY: General Assembly called upon U.S.S.R. and Hungary to desist from repressive measures
Dec. 12	NATURAL RESOURCES: General Assembly established commission to survey rights of peoples to sovereignty over their natural resources
Dec. 12	FREEDOM OF INSORMATION: General Assembly recommended that Members open their countries to greater freedom of communication about the U.N.
Dec. 12	ECONOMIC DEVELOPMENT: General Assembly adopted nine resolutions including requests for studies of means for stimulating private investment, establishment of a roster of technical personnel and means for improving international commodity trade
Dec. 12	PALESTINE: General Assembly reiterated concern for plight of refugees and precarious financial position of UNRWA
Dec. 12	MEMBERSHIP: Guinea admitted as 82nd Member
Dec. 12	NON-SELF-GOVERNING TERRITORIES: General Assembly urged administering authorities to give constant attention to questions of racial discrimination
Dec. 12	NON-SELF-GOVERNING TERRITORIES: Committee on Information from Non-Self-Governing Territories continued for three years
Dec. 13	BUDGET: $91,861,170 authorized—$6,059,050 for 1958, $60,-802,120 for 1959 and $25,000,000 for UNEF
Dec. 13	OUTER SPACE: General Assembly established Ad Hoc Study Group
Dec. 13	RADIATION: Scientific Committee continued
Dec. 13	HUNGARY: Credentials Committee of General Assembly took no action on the credentials of the Hungarian delegation
Dec. 13	ALGERIA: General Assembly unable to agree on a resolution
Dec. 18	ARMS CONTROL: last meeting of Conference of Experts on Surprise Attack
Dec. 29	ECONOMIC COMMISSION FOR AFRICA: first session

INDEX

Each entry below contains references to specific dates in the *Chronology,* rather than to page numbers. This does not make any item more difficult to find and provides a quick picture of the chronological development under each subject heading (for example, see *vetoes*).

The reference under the first heading, *Administrative* Committee on Coordination is—1946: S 21—and means that the event took place on September 21, 1946.

Administrative Committee on
  Co-ordination
  1946: S 21
Administrative Tribunal
  1949: N 24, D 9
  1954: Jl 13
Aerial Incident Cases
  1956: Mr 14
  1957: Q 16
  1958: Ag 22
Afghanistan
  1946: N 19
Africa, See also Algeria, Egypt, Ghana,
  Guinea, Morocco, Sudan, Southwest
  Africa, Togoland, Tunisia, Union of
  S. Africa, United Arab Republic
  1958: Ap 29, D 29
Albania, see also Corfu Channel
  1949: Ap 9, D 15
  1954: Jl 15
  1955: D 14
Algeria
  1955: S 20, N 25
  1956: Jl 26
  1957: F 15, D 10
  1958: D 13
Ambatieles Case
  1952: Jl 1
  1953: My 19
Anglo-Norwegian Fisheries Case
  1951: D 18
Antarctica Cases
  1956: Mr. 16
Apartheid (see also Union of
  South Africa).
  1950: D 2
  1957: Ja 30
  1958: O 23
Arctic Inspection Zone
  1958: My 2
Argentina
  1956: Mr. 16
Arms control (see also Atomic Energy)
  1946: D 14
  1947: F 13, Ap 30
  1948: Ja 22
  1949: O 11, 18

1952: Ja 11, Ap 15, My 28
1953: Ap 8, N 28
1954: Ap 9, My 13, Jl 20
1955: F 25, My 9, Je 1, Jl 23, Ag 29,
  S 13, O 21, N 23
Asylum case
  1950: N 20, 27
  1951: Je 13
Atlantic Charter
  1941: Ag 14
Atomic energy, see also Radiation
  1945: Ag 6, N 15, D 16
  1946: Ja 24, Je 14, Je 19, S 26, D 31
  1947: S 11
  1948: Mr 30, Je 22, O 2, N 4
  1949: Jl 29, N 23
  1953: D 8
  1954: D 4
  1955: Ag 8, D 3
  1956: Ap 18, S 20
  1957: Jl 29
  1958: My 7, S 1
Atomic testing
  1958: Ap 30
Austria
  1955: D 14

Bacteriological warfare
  1952: Jl 3; 9
  1953: Ap 23
Balkans (see also Greece)
  1952: Ja 23, 31
  1954: Ag 1
Barcelona Light & Power case
  (Belgium vs. Spain)
  1958: S 23
Belgium
  1957: Ag 2, N 27
  1958: S 23
Berlin
  1958: O 25
  1949: My 4, 12
Bernadotte, Folke, Count
  1948: Mr 20, S 17
  1950: Je 14
Budget
  1946: D 14

41

1947: N 20
1948: D 11
1949: D 10
1950: D 15
1951: D 21
1952: D 21
1953: D 9
1954: D 17
1955: D 16
1956: D 21
1957: D 14
1958: Je 30, D 13
Bulgaria
1949: O 22
1950: Mr 30, Jl 18
1955: D 14
1957: D 16
Burma
1948: Ap 19
1953: Ap 23, D 8
1954: O 29

Cambodia
1955: D 14
Cameroons (French)
1957: Ap 16
1958: D 5
Cartography
1955: F 15
Ceylon
1955: D 14
Charter
1945: Je 26, Jl 6, Ag 8, O 24
1955: Je 20, D 16
1957: N 26
Children
1946: D 11
1947: Ag 8
1948: O 1, D 3
1949: N 18
1950: D 1
1953: O 6
1957: D 31
Chile
1956: Mr 16
China (representation)
1950: S 29
1951:F 13, N 13
1952: O 25
1953: S 15
1954: S 21
1955: F 3, S 20
1956: N 16
1957: S 24
1959: S 23
China (bombing)

1950: S 12
Collective Measures Committee
1951: Mr 5
Commodities
1950: O 25
1954: Ag 5
1955: O 3, 26
1958: S 8, 11, 22
Communications, see also Transport and
   Communications
Conservation
1949: Ag 17
Copper
1958: S 8
Corfu Channel case
1947: Ja 10, Mr 25, Ap 9
1949: Ap 19, D 15
Criminal jurisdiction
1951: Ag 1
1953: Jl 27
Cyprus
1955: S 23
1957: F 26, D 14
1958: D 5
Czechoslovakia
1948: My 24
1956: Mr 14

Devastated areas, see Reconstruction
Dixon, Owen, Sir
1950: Ap 12
Dumbarton Oaks
1944: O 9
Duties of states
1950: N 17
Economic and Social Council
1946: Ja 28, My 25, S 11
1947: F 28, Jl 19
1948: F 2, Jl 19
1949: F 7, Jl 5
1950: F 7, Jl 3, O 12
1951: F 20, Jl 30, D 18
1952: Mr 24, My 20, D 16
1953: Mr 31, Je 30, N 30
1954: Mr 30, Je 29, N 5
1955: Mr 29, My 16, Jl 15, D 5
1956: Ap 17, Jl 9, D 17
1957: Ap 16, Jl 2, D 10
1958: Ap 15, Jl 1, O 23, D 10

Economic Commission for Africa
1958: Ap 29, D 29
Economic Commission for Asia and the
   Far East
1947: Mr 28, Je 16
Economic Commission for Europe
1947: Mr 28, My 2

42

Economic Commision for Latin America
1948: F 25
Economic development, see also
International Finance
Organization, Special United
Nations Fund for Economic
Development
1951: F 19
1952: Ja 12, Je 23
1953: Ap 23, D 7
1954: My 13, Ag 10, D 11
1955: Mr 7, D 9
1957: F 26, D 14
1958: D 12
Education
1947: N 17
Egypt, see also United Arab Republic
1947: Jl 8
1950: Mr 2
1956: N 12, 18, 20
Employment
1946: F 16
1947: Ja 20, Je 2
1949: O 22
1951: S 18
Eritrea
1949: N 21
1950: D 2
1952: S 11

Federation of Malaya
1957: S 17
Field of Observers, Panel of
1950: N 3
1952: Ja 23
Field Service
1949: N 22
1950: Mr 1
Finland
1955: D 14
Fiscal
1946: O 1
1947: My 19
1954: Ag 5
Flag
1947: O 20
Forced labour, see labour
France
1950: Mr 2
1952: Ag 27, D 19
1956: O 30, N 7, 24, D 5, 22
1957: Ap 16, Jl 6
1958: Je 18
Freedom of Information
1946: Je 21
1947: F 10, My 19

1948: Mr 23
1950: Ag 9
1952: Mr 3, D 16

General Agreement on Tariff and Trade
1947: O 30
1955: Mr 7
General Assembly, see also Interim
Committee
1946: Ja 10, O 22
1947: Ap 28, S 16
1948: Ap 16, S 21
1949: Ap 5, S 20
1950: S 19
1951: N 6
1952: O 14
1953: F 24, Ag 17, S 15
1954: Ja 10, S 20, S 21
1955: S 20
1956: N 1, 4, 12
1957: Mr 8, S 10, 17
1958: Ag 8, S 16
Genocide
1948: D 9
1951: Ja 12, My 28
Germany
1951: D 20
1952: Ag 5
1955: Ag 1
Ghana
1957: Mr 8
Graham, Frank P.
1951: Mr 30
Greece, see also Balkans, Cyprus
1946: Ja 21, Ag 24, S 20, D 3, 19
1947: Je 25, Jl 29, Ag 19, S 15, O 21
1948: N 27
1949: N 18
1950: D 1
1952: Ja 31, D 17
1954: Ag 1   ,
Guatemala
1954: Je 20
Guinea
1958: D 12
Hammarskjold, Dag
1952: Ap 10
Headquarters
1946: F 14, Mr 21, Ag 16, D 14
1947: Je 26, N 20
1948: Mr 23
1950: Ag 21
1952: F 27
1958: Mr 3
Health
1946: Je 19

Hoffman, Paul G.
  1958: D 4
Honduras
  1958: Jl 1
Human Rights
  1946: F 16
  1947: Ja 27, F 10
  1948: D 9, 10
  1950: D 4
  1951: Ja 12, My 28
  1952: F 4
  1953: N 28
  1954: D 4
  1955: D 2
  1956: D 13
  1957: O 11, N 13
  1958: O 16, N 14
Hungary
  1947: Ap 22
  1949: O 22
  1950: Mr 30, Jl 18
  1954: Jl 12
  1955: D 14
  1956: O 28, N 4
  1957: O 16, D 9, 21
  1958: Je 21, Jl 14, D 12, 13
Hydrogen bomb
  1952: N 1

Iceland
  1946: N 19
India, see also Kashmir
  1955: D 22
Indians in the Union of South Africa
  1949: My 14
  1950: D 2
  1957: Ja 30
Indonesia
  1946: Ja 21
  1947: Jl 30, Ag 1, 25
  1948: Ja 17, D 24
  1949: Ja 28, My 7, Ag 23, D 13, 27
  1950: S 28
  1951: Mr 14, Ap 3
Information, see also Freedom of
     information
  1958: F 26
Inter-governmental Maritime
     Consultative Organization
  1948: F 19
  1958: Mr 17
Interhandel case
  1957: O 2
Interim Committee of the General
     Assembly
  1947: N 13

International Court of Justice
  1945: Ap 3
  1946: F 6, Ap 3
  1947: Ap 9
  1948: My 28, Jl 28
  1949: Ap 9, 11, O 22, D 6, 15
  1950: Mr 2, 3, 29, Jl 11, 18, N 20, 27
  1951: My 28, Je 13, Jl 5, D 18
  1952: Jl 1, 22, A 27
  1953: My 19, N 17, 18
  1954: F 18, Ap 2, Je 15, Jl 12, 13,
     N 23
  1955: Ap 6, Je 7, D 3, 22
  1956: Mr 14, 16, Je 1
  1957: Jl 6, O 2, 10, 16, N 27
  1958: Jl 1, Ag 22, S 23
International Finance Corporation
  1951: F 18
  1954: D 11
  1955: Ap 15, N 3
  1956: Jl 24
  1957: F 20
International Law
  1946: D 11
  1947: My 12, N 21
  1949: Ap 11, D 1
  1958: F 24, Je 10, D 10
International Refugee Organization
  1948: N 18
  1952: Ja 31
International Trade Organization
  1947: N 21
  1948: Mr 24
Iran
  1946: Ja 19
  1951: Jl 5
  1952: Jl 22
Iraq
  1958: Jl 14
Ireland
  1955: D 14
Israel, see also Palestine
  1948: My 14
  1949: My 11
  1956: O 29, 30, N 7, 24
  1957: O 10
Italy
  1949: N 21
  1950: N 21
  1950: D 2, 15

Japan
  1954: Ap 2
  1956: D 18
Jarring, Gunnar
  1957: F 20, Ap 29

Jerusalem
  1949: D 9
  1950: D 15
Jordan
  1955: D 14
  1956: D 16
  1958: Jl 17, Ag 21, S 29, N 2

Kashmir
  1947: N 14
  1948: Ja 20, Ap 21, Ag 13
  1949: Ja 1, Mr 21
  1950: Mr 14, Ap 12, S 15
  1951: Ap 30, N 10
  1952: Ja 31, D 23
  1953: Mr 23
  1957: Ja 24, F 20, Ap 29, D 2
  1959: Mr 31
Korea
  1947: N 14
  1948: My 10, Je 25, D 12
  1949: O 21
  1950: Je 15, 27, Jl 7, 31, S 6, O 7,
    N 5, 30, D 1, 12, 14, 23
  1951: F 1, My 18, Je 29, Jl 1, 10,
    16, N 27
  1952: D 3, 22
  1953: Ap 11, Je 8, Jl 27, 30, Ag 5,
    28, S 11, 24, D 3, 7
  1954: Ja 23, Ap 26, D 10
  1955: Ja 5, Ag 4, D 31
  1957: N 26, 29
  1958: N 14

Labour
  1951: Mr 19
  1953: D 7
Laos
  1955: D 14
Law of the Sea
  1958: F 24, D 10
Lead
  1958: S 11
League of Nations
  1946: Ap 8, Ag 1, N 19
  1953: O 23
Lebanon
  1946: F 4
  1949: Mr 23
  1958: My 22, Je 11, Jl 15, 18, 21,
    Ag 21, 26, S 20, 29, O 25, D 9
Legan Personality of the U.N.
  1949: Ap 11, D 1
Libya
  1949: N 21, D 10
  1950: D 15

1951: Mr 29, D 24
1955: D 14
1958: D 10
Lie, Trygve
  1946: F 1
  1950: Je 6, O 12
  1952: N 10
Liechtenstein
  1950: Mr 29

Malaya, see Federation of Malaya
McCloy, John J.
  1956: N 24
Membership
  1946: Ja 25, Je 24, Jl 2, 8, Ag 2, 3,
    9, 29, N 19, D 15
  1947: Ap 22, My 7, Jl 2, 10, 26, Ag
    15, 18, 19, 21, S 19, 30, O 1
  1948: Ap 10, 18, 19, My 28, D 15
  1949: Ap 8, 18, 19, My 28, D 15
  1950: Mr 3, S 28
  1952: F 6, S 16, 18, 19
  1955: D 13, 14, 15
  1956: N 12, D 18
  1957: Mr 8, S 8, 9, 17
  1959: D 12
Middle East, see also Palestine
  1958: Jl 19, Ag 13
Military Staff Committee
  1946: F 4
  1947: Ap 30
Minorities
  1947: F 10
Minquires-Ecrehos Islands
  1953: N 17
Missing Persons
  1950: Mr 15
  1952: Ja 24, O 1
Morocco
  1952: Ag 27, D 19
  1955: D 3
  1956: N 12

Narcotic Drugs
  1946: F 16, N 19
  1947: Jl 24
  1948: O 8
  1953: My 11
Natural resources
  1949: Ag 17
  1958: D 12
Nepal
  1955: D 14
Netherlands
  1955: D 15
  1957: Jl 1, N 27

New Guinea, see also West Irian
Nicaragua
  1958: Jl 1
Nimitz, Chester W.
  1949: Mr 21
Non-self-governing territories
  1946: F 9, D 14
  1952: D 10
  1953: N 27
  1955: D 15
  1957: Ag 2, N 26
  1958: D 12
Non-governmental organizations
  1946: Je 12
  1950: F 27
Norway
  1951: D 18
  1957: Jl 6
Nottebohm case
  1953: N 18
  1954: Ap 6
Nurnberg
  1946: D 11

Obscene publications
  1948: D 3
Olive oil
  1955: O 3
Olympio, Sylvanus E.
  1947: D 8
Organization for Trade Co-operation
  1957: N 26
Outer space
  1958: D 13

Pacific settlement of disputes
  1949: Ap 28, D 1
Pakistan, see also Kashmir
  1947: S 30
Palestine
  1947: Ap 2, My 15, Ag 31, N 29
  1948: Mr 5, Ap 1, 16, 23, My 14,
    15, 20, 22, 29, Je 11, 15, Jl 15,
    S 17, N 19, D 11
  1949: F 24, Mr 23, Ap 3, Jl 20,
    Ag 11, D 8, 9
  1950: Je 14, N 17, D 14, 15
  1951: My 8, 18
  1952: Ja 26, N 6
  1953: O 27, N 24, 27
  1954: Ja 22
  1955: Mr 29, S 8, N 2
  1956: Ap 17, O 13
  1957 D 16
  1958: Ja 18, O 27, D 8, 12
Panel of field of observers,

  see Field Observers
Peace Observation Group
  1950: N 3
  1952: Ja 23
Pearson, Lester
  1952: Mr 13
Population
  1946: O 3
  1947: F 6
  1954: Ag 31
Portugal
  1955: D 14, 22
Postal administration
  1950: N 16
  1951: Mr 28, O 24
Preparatory Commission of the U.N.
  1945: Je 27, Ag 16, N 24
Prisoners of war
  1950: D 14
  1953: Ap 11, Je 8, Ag 5, S 10, 24,
    D 3, 7
Puerto Rico
  1953: N 27

Radiation, see also Atomic energy
  1955: D 3
  1956: Ap 9
  1957: Ap 8, N 14
  1958: Ja 27, Ag 10, D 13
Reconstruction
  1946: Je 21, Jl 29
Refugees
  1946: D 15
  1948: N 18
  1949: D 3
  1950: D 14
  1951: Ja 1, Jl 2, 25
  1952: Ja 31, Mr 1
  1954: Ap 22, O 21
  1957: N 26
  1958: Ap 30, O 27, D 5
Regional Offices
  1947: Mr 28, My 2, Je 16
  1948: F 25
  1957: D 14
  1958: D 29
Rockefeller, John D.
  1946: D 14
Romania
  1949: O 22
  1950: Mr 30, Jl 18
  1955: D 14
  1957: O 16
San Marino
  1954: F 18
Scheyven, Raymond

46

1953: D 7
1954: My 13, Ag 10, D 11
1955: Mr 7
Secretary-General of the U.N.
 1946: F 1
 1949: N 22, D 1
 1950: Mr 1, Je 6, Jl 18, O 12, N 20
 1952: N 10
 1953: Mr 13, Ap 10, D 14
 1954: D 10
 1956: N 4, 8, 16, 20
 1957: D 16
 1958: Ja 18, Mr 6, Jl 19, Ag 21, S 29
Security Council, see also Vetoes
 1945: F 4, Je 7
 1946: Ja 17
 1949: Ap 14
Slavery
 1953: O 23
 1956: S 7
Social
 1946: F 16, D 14
 1947: Ja 20, F 4
 1949: N 17
 1950: D 1
Somaliland
 1949: N 21
 1950: D 2, 15
Southwest Africa
 1946: D 14
 1947: N 1
 1948: N 26
 1949: Jl 11, D 6
 1950: Jl 11, D 13
 1952: Ja 19
 1952: Ja 19
 1953: N 28
 1954: O 11, N 23
 1955: Je 7, D 3
 1956: Je 1
 1957: Ja 23, F 26, O 25
 1958: O 30
Spain
 1946: Ap 8, Je 18, 26, D 12
 1950: N 4
 1955: D 14
 1958: S 23
Special U.N. Fund for Economic
  Development
 1952: Ja 12, J 2, 23
 1953: Ap 23, D 7
 1954: My 13, Ag 10, D 11
 1955: Mr 7, D 9
Specialized agencies
 1946: S 21, D 14
 1947: N 15

1948: N 18
1951: D 20
Statelessness
 1954: S 13
Statistics
 1946: F 16
 1947: Ja 27, S 8
Sudan
 1956: N 12
 1958: F 22
Suez
 1950: S 16
 1951: S 1
 1954: Mr 29
 1956: O 13, 30, 31, N 2, 4, 7, 8; 16;
   18, 20, 21, 24, D 22, 28
 1957: F 2, D 14
Sugar
 1958: S 22
Surinam
 1955: D 15
Sweden
 1946: N 19
 1957: Jl 10, N 27
Switzerland
 1957: O 2
Syria
 1946: F 4
 1958: Mr 6

Technical Assistance
 1948: D 4
 1949: Ag 15, N 16
 1950: Je 12
 1951: N 5
 1952: F 6
 1953: F 26, N 12
 1954: N 26
 1955: O 26
 1956: O 17
 1957: O 10
 1958: Mr 11, O 16, D 4
Thailand
 1946: D 15
 1954: Je 18
Tin
 1950: O 25
Togoland (British)
 1955: D 15
 1956: My 9
Togoland (French)
 1947: D 8
 1955: D 16
 1956: O 23
 1957: D 14
 1958: Ap 27, O 13

Trade
1947: O 30, N 21
1948: Mr 24
1957: N 26
Traffic in Persons
1949: D 2
1951: Jl 25
Transport
1946: F 16
1947: F 6
1948: F 19
1949: Ag 23
1952: Mr 26
1953: D 20
1954: My 11
1958: Mr 17
Trieste
1947: Ja 10, S 24
Trusteeship
1946: D 13
1947: Mr 26, Ap 2, 24
1948: F 18, Ap 21, Je 16, Jl 6, N 18
1949: Ja 24, Je 15, S 27, N 15, D 8
1950: Ja 19, Je 1, D 18
1951: Ja 30, Je 5, D 18
1952: Ja 18, F 27, Je 3, N 19, D 21
1953: Je 16
1954: Ja 28, Je 2
1955: Ja 25, Je 8, O 24, D 15, 16
1956: F 7, Je 7, My 9, O 23, D 10
1957: Ap 16, Mr 24, My 20, S 12,
     D 14
1958: Ja 30, Ap 27, Je 9, S 15, O 13,
     N 6, D 5
Tunisia
1952: Ap 14, Je 20, D 17
1953: N 11
1954: D 17
1956: N 12
1958: F 18, Je 4, Jl 18
Twenty Year Peace Program
1950: N 20

Union of South Africa
1946: D 8
1949: My 14
1950: D 2
1952: D 5
1953: D 8
1957: Ja 30, N 26
1958: O 30
U.S.S.R.
1950: Ja 13, Ag 1
1956: Mr 14
United Arab Republic
1958: Mr 6, My 22, Jl 17

United Kingdom, see also Corfu,
     Cyprus, Togoland
1951: D 18
1956: Mr 16, O 30, N 7, 24, D 22
1957: O 16
1958: Jl 18
U.N. Emergency Force
1956: N 5, 10, 12, 15
United States
1952: Ag 27
1953: N 27
1957: O 2, 16
1958: Jl 15, 18, Ag 13
Uniting for Peace Resolution
1950: N 3
van Heuven Goodhart, G. J.
1950: D 14
Vetoes
1946: F 16, Je 18, 26, Ag 29, S 20
1947: Mr 25, Jl 29, Ag 18, 19, 21, 25,
     S 15, 24, O 1
1948: Ap 10, My 24, Je 22, Ag 18,
     O 25, D 13
1949: Ap 8, S 7, 13, O 11, 18, D 13
1950: S 6, 12, O 12, N 30
1952: F 6, Jl 3, 9, S 16, 18, 19
1953: Mr 13
1954: Ja 22, Mr 29, Je 18, 20
1955: D 13, 14, 15
1956: O 13, 30, N 4
1957: F 20, S 9
1958: My 2, Jl 18
Wellington Conference
1944: N 1
West Irian
1954: D 10
1955: D 19
1957: F 28, N 29
Wheat
1955: O 26
Wheller, R. A.
1956: N 24
Women
1946: Je 21
1947: F 10
1948: D 3
1952: D 20
1954: Jl 7
1957: F 20
1958: Ag 11
World Health Organization
1946: Je 19
Yemen
1947: S 30
Yugoslavia
1951: D 14